DOUBLING BACK

Ten paths trodden in memory

DOUBLING BACK

Ten paths trodden in memory

Linda Cracknell

First published May 2014

Freight Books
49-53 Virginia Street
Glasgow, G1 1TS
www.freightbooks.co.uk

A CIP catalogue reference for this book is available from the British Library

ISBN 978-1-908754-54-7
eISBN 978-1-908755-5-4

Typeset by Freight in Garamond
Printed and bound by PB Print, Czech Republic

the publisher acknowledges investment from
Creative Scotland toward the publication of this book

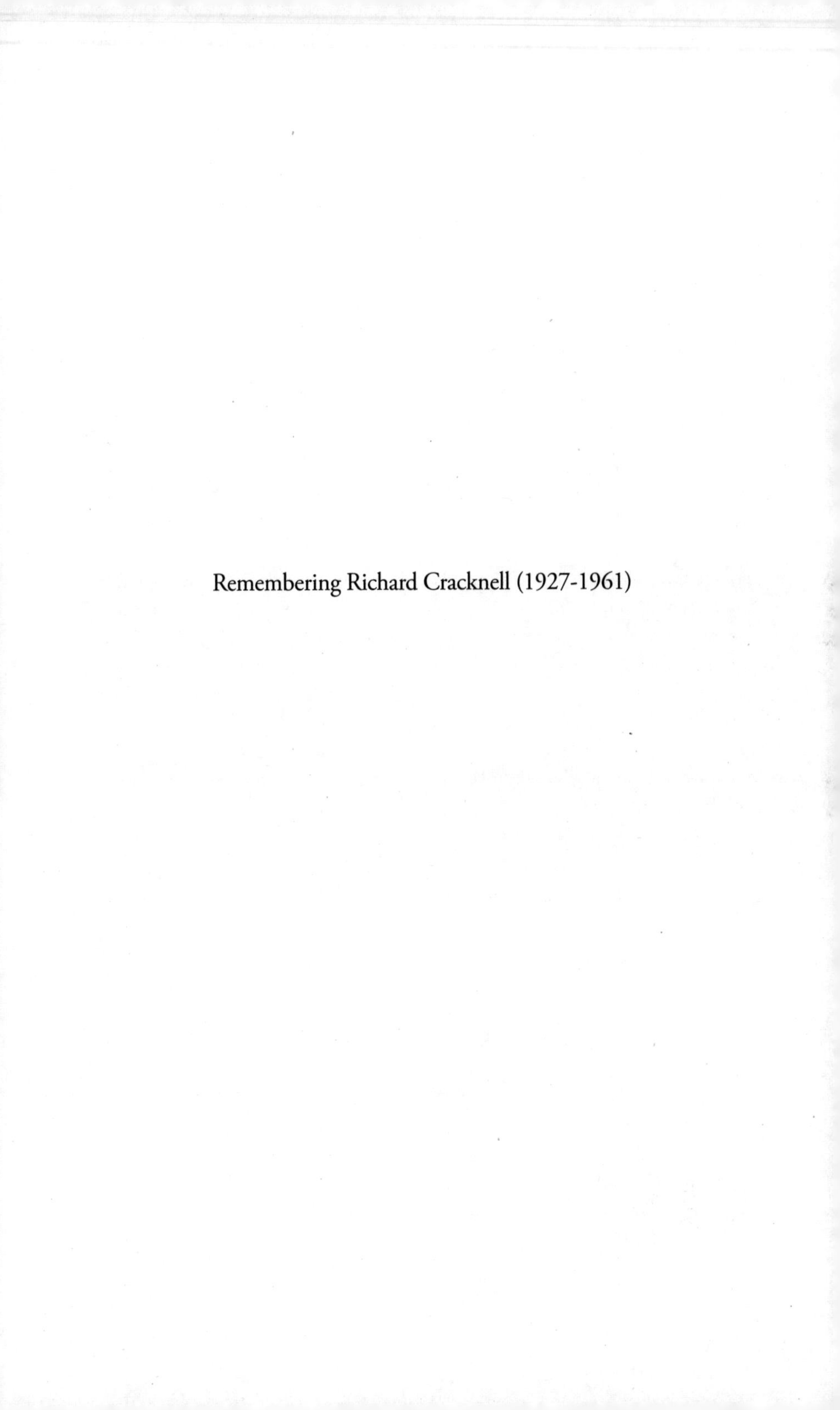

Remembering Richard Cracknell (1927-1961)

Contents

Pappa's Shoes
A Wartime escape route, Norway

Dancing, Kicking up her Legs
A hillside near Abriachan, Loch Ness

The Return of Hoof Beats
Newtonmore to Kirkmichael
Cairngorms, Scotland

Friendly Paths
The Birks of Aberfeldy
Perthshire, Scotland

The Opening Door
Boscastle, Cornwall

Outlasting our Tracks
Finsteraarhorn, Bernese Oberland, Switzerland

Stairway to Heaven?
Rellen to Valle Laguart
Alicante, Spain

Baring our Soles
Ndumberi Village
Central Kenya

The Dog's Route
A drove road between
Perthshire and the Isle
of Skye, Scotland
To be a Pilgrim
Saint Cuthbert's Way
Melrose to Lindisfarne

Saunters

Château de Lavigny, Switzerland, August 2012

The desk at the window of my room overlooks the orderly lawns of the Château. Hibiscus is flowering on the veranda and roses are trained over arches. A few kilometres below, Lác Leman shimmers, and beyond it rises the hazy outline of the Alps. A huge plane tree flapped its leaves close to my window throughout last night, played into tunes by the wind and rain. I arrived three days ago to a heat-wave but thunderstorms are beginning to fracture it now; the air is cooled by rain and then rises up yet more steamily when the sun returns.

I'm here on a writing retreat, and each day for a month is my own. Already I have established rituals. I like to be first to the kitchen, to collect the fresh loaves left hanging on the little side-door which opens onto the village street. After a glass of orange juice, I put on my shoes and slip into the garden, past the lavender bushes fussed over by small white butterflies and scrambling with bees. At the bottom of the sloping lawn, a wicket gate opens into the wider world.

At first the way is familiar. There's a grassy avenue between a field of sunflowers to my left, each swinging heavy heads in the same direction, and rows of glossy vines to my right. Soon though, I'll break new ground, perhaps venturing into the wooded slopes of the Aubonne valley to find out where a set of steps go that lead intriguingly upwards.

Greeting the day like this I walk the restlessness out of my body and wake up to my work. But my morning walks here are also about exploring. It's as if the Château is laced into place by small lanes, tracks and paths between farms and villages. I need to get to know them, to fill in the detail of my circle a little more each day. There are places to go back to, perhaps to sit and draw, or just for the pleasure of returning. By walking an hour each morning, I plant myself here.

My internal monologue and a tiny hand-stitched notebook always accompany me. There may be chatter or observations I need to note down, a new story idea, or solutions to my writing problems. It's as if I think better on the move, think more creatively, or as Jean-Jacques Rousseau would have it, 'my mind only works with my legs'. Slow but alert. Attentive to both inner and outer landscapes. Later, each walk will become a journal entry and a sketch map.

The first time I remember striking out alone on a journey I can't have been more than about four years old, yet many of the elements of my adult walking are reflected in it. There was something deliberate about it, a necessary adventure which changed my relationship to a landscape. It remains greenly luminous in my memory.

After the death of my father in 1961, my mother moved my older sister, brother and myself to a Surrey suburb. I was under two, and the garden became my habitat. It was where I went by choice but also where I was banished. My mother would turn the key on the inside while she washed the kitchen floor. In memory, although we disagree about this now, the key then stayed turned for much of the day.

As the corner plot of an estate of circularly-arranged houses, it was by default a large garden stretching down to the railway line running between Guildford and Waterloo. Whilst tipping its hat to tameness and family life with lawns for somersaults, handstands and sunbathing and a vegetable garden where my mother teased up rows of beans and blackcurrants, it was the remainder that most interested me, where things grew of their own accord. Down one side of the garden and across its end a dense jungle of bracken and rhododendron, swayed over by silver birch, encroached on the order. A rowan tree hosted enormous pigeons when loaded with fruit. I would sometimes pick the berries, crush them with ditch-water and serve the resulting 'tea' in old yoghurt pots to my imaginary guests. They came to visit at the 'dwelling' I built in the woods out of old timber packing cases.

The garden teemed with life and mysteries. I was secure between its taut wire fences, but it also offered exploration and adventure and I became myself amidst the undergrowth and mud. The ground was clayey, crossed by drainage ditches that emptied into a larger one stinking its way parallel with the railway line. Leaves darkened these ditches and the water was covered with a film of oily rust. The sludginess always fascinated me and drew me down into them.

My first solo journey wasn't exactly a walk but rather a crawl on hands and knees, a traverse parallel to the railway line from one boundary fence to the other at the bottom of the garden. I never saw my mother in this part of the garden except when she emptied grass clippings onto the compost heap, but some impulse sent me trail-blazing a tunnel though a forest of sappy bracken. My hands dragged through leaf mould, sinking into mysterious layers of damp things, too soft to exactly be considered ground. I disturbed dark smells, slugs and worms. I pressed on, despite slow progress across the no-mans-land, determined to reach my destination. In memory the journey took a long morning.

When I completed the expedition, I recall a sense of achievement; a new, braver me had emerged at the other end. It was play of sorts I suppose, but serious-feeling play, and solitary. I repeated it and I discovered other journeys to make in the garden, wearing paths through the undergrowth that came to carry our family stories. Supposedly I often disappeared like this, only traceable by the quiver of bracken fronds, and emerging muddy and beetle-infested a few hours later.

It was also in that area of the garden that my hands scrabbled below the surface for treasures, churning up fragments of pottery, and one day, a large white shiny lump that I dragged onto the lawn for inspection. It turned out to be a smashed ceramic insulator from the railway line, but this did nothing to dispel the thrill of my own act of discovery.

This exhilarating place could also turn on me. There were brambles, stinging nettles, poisonous berries. I remember once sitting damp-bottomed and submerged amongst the undergrowth when I saw something from the corner of my eye. Whatever it was, the horror of it propelled me towards the house screaming, yet unable to explain what I'd seen. I only knew that it was too terrifying to revisit or give words to. I can vaguely remember it now. Something was caught in my hair or perhaps in a nearby branch and blurred by proximity; the suggestion of a spider's web shape but with a great darkness and weight and horrible stickiness.

The garden was where I went to sob away my private miseries but also a setting for odd rituals. At a predestined time each day, I'd climb onto a pile of silver-birch logs, swallow a lungful of air and bellow across the adjoining back gardens the repeated line from Cilla Black's, 'Anyone Who Had a Heart'; number one in the charts in 1964.

I suspect I was a strange child, internalised, tearful, quiet. But I remember that there was always a lot going on in my imagination. It was fed by this strange Surrey garden that was a place of safety, adventure, play and enchantment, with a geography that came to be mapped intricately in my head as I grew higher than the bracken. I learnt about my need to discover, to make sense of local geography by propelling myself through it. I trod routes into familiarity, let my imagination work on the things left behind by others, and got the dirt of the place under my fingernails. I found self reliance and independence there.

My mother married again when I was eight, to Hugh, and we'd take a weekly drive out of Surrey suburbia, seeking splashes of green, lungfuls of fresh air, a stretch of our legs. We'd go to Cookham to look for cowslips in the Spring; or to the Downs and Stanley Spencer's decorated chapel at Burghclere; or to Hugh's beloved chalky ways near the Thames in Berkshire.

I was always the one screaming 'wait for me' from several yards behind on family walks. I was the 'Cry Baby Bunting' whose 'Daddy's gone a-hunting', seemingly always torn between wanting to be alone and fury at being left out. I'm not sure what, apart from being the youngest, made me so slow. At school I often won the 100 Yard sprint. I wonder now if it was because I stopped to look at bugs or to poke a stick in a hole in the ground, dwelling upon wonders along the way.

The word 'dwell' now seems appropriate. Its etymology contains the idea of a trance induced by a narcotic berry, being led astray, and finally through hindering or delaying to lingering and thus to 'making a home'. The word suggests edges of error – the danger zone where creativity often happens – and the idea of home and security. All inherent in my 'dwelling' in the thickest undergrowth of the garden where I began to be an explorer.

I've remained both a daily walker and an 'expedition' walker. My life has been shaped by it to some extent. An enjoyment of walking in remote and mountainous terrain explains at least in part my move to Scotland in 1990 from where I started to write five years later.

The walks in this collection have been made over the last eight years. They are mostly retreadings of past trails either taken by myself or others. In the act of doubling back I discover what remains or is new and listen for memories, some of which have become buried. I also explore how the act of walking and the landscapes we move through can shape who we are and how we understand the world.

These are ambles, treks and expeditions ranging across mountains, valleys and coasts in Scotland, Kenya, Spain, Cornwall, Norway and here in Switzerland. Each setting out is the realisation of an obsessive curiosity and seems to have chosen me, rather as stories choose to be written. Sometimes they have similarly unforeseen resolutions.

I think of these first two walks as 'saunters' because they are musing and exploratory. Neither of them are steady lines between two places, but meandering rambles with opportunities for distraction and deviation. They take me to places significant in the early lives of Thomas Hardy and Jessie Kesson, landscapes that had long legacies beyond the writers' youthful roamings and inspired their later texts. I'm also following my younger self. I want to explore how the freedom of certain places at significant points in our lives can encourage us to become close observers of the world, or transform our imaginations, or simply, transform us.

The Opening Door

North
Beeny Cliff
Penally
Meachard
Valency River
BOSCASTLE
Minster Church

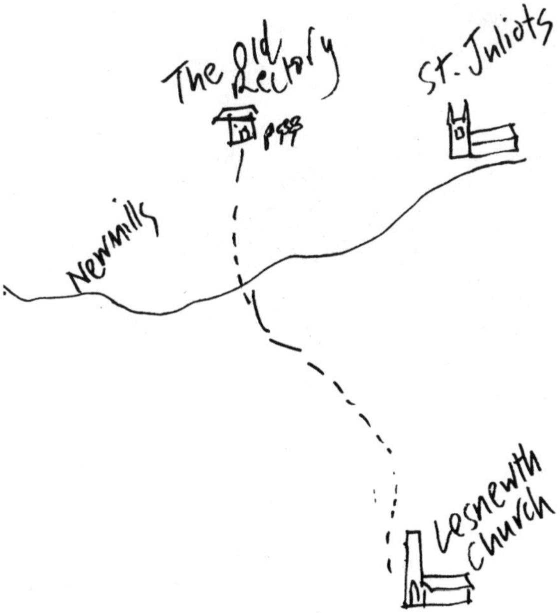

The Old Rectory

St. Juliots

Newmills

Lesnewth Church

Boscastle, Cornwall

When I set out for Lyonesse,
A Hundred miles away,
The rime was on the spray,
And starlight lit my lonesomeness
When I set out for Lyonesse
A hundred miles away.
From *When I set out for Lyonesse* (1870), Thomas Hardy

The sea always draws me, especially where cliffs soar and plummet and birds are like shooting stars against dark rocky chasms. I'm at Boscastle in Cornwall, with a salt tang in my nostrils. The rhythmic company of wash and breaker, and the estuaries tamed by the retreating tide into mud flats seem to remind me of something. Perhaps it's my sea-faring ancestors, the Drakes and Chichesters, who from 50 miles east of here at Braunton ran the last sailing coasters of the early 20th century, delivering coal and slate.

But for now I turn my back on Penally Point, the gnarled headland that guards the serpentine entrance to Boscastle harbour. I leave the view out to the surf-skirted black bulk of Meachard to which ships too large to navigate into the harbour were once moored. I turn away from salt towards freshwater.

The Valency Valley beckons me inland, eastwards, across what I remember was a meadow behind the row of shops, and is now a car park. The ground is tightly netted and gabionned against the vandal-fingers of water. I'm soon walking through an aisle of trees, alone on a quiet path that follows the north bank of the river. A duck flies low and fast ahead of me, embodying purpose. Like the jets I see skimming lochs at home, it adjusts its angle in expert increments to steer the central course of the winding river, then disappears around a bend. But this flight defines the landscape as miniature; a narrow valley with secret corners. A scale and nature that I'm here to re-learn.

The area of land defined by these waters and paths has swayed the course of English literature, and also shaped my own track. At least one love story gleams within its lush green crevices.

In 1976 I arrived in Boscastle for a week's painting holiday with the sullen steps of a post-glandular-fever, first-time-in-love seventeen year old. 'I've got here but feel terribly lonely and depressed,' I complained to my diary on the first night. 'Everyone is so cheerful and friendly but I'm very isolated. It always takes me so long to get used to a place.'

Bringing with me a 1:50,000 Ordnance Survey map and an instinct for exploration and recovery, I was soon enchanted. Over the week, letters to my boyfriend became less frequent as I wrote more lengthily in my diary, and at the end I complained: 'I really wish I could stay another week, to go on some more walks, and meet more people... I can just imagine waking up in the mornings to seeing the garden through the window [at home] rather than the sun and the sea and the hills and the cottages and friendliness. ...I find it hard to believe that all the people I've met here have been purely through myself. ...' In that week I had the sensation of tumbling into my adult life – discovering I was someone who loved to be alone, to be gregarious, to make connections through reading, and to affiliate myself to a place of raw beauty through the movement of my feet.

I learnt from Tom, a bespectacled literature lover also staying at my guest house, that Thomas Hardy had come here as a young architect in 1870 and fallen in love with Emma Lavinia Gifford. At first out of politeness I listened to what Tom had to say, aware of his wife and sister-in-law rolling their eyes behind him. Once drawn into the tale, I also leafed through the books he offered and indulged his recitals of Hardy's poetry, such as *The Seven Times*: 'I thought not that I should meet an eyesome maiden,/But found one there'.

Emma was a young woman above Hardy's social status. An unconventional spirit took her exploring on horseback the thrusting black cliff tops, hanging valleys, and the waterfalls in the deep centre of this landscape. Her father's church of St Juliot's and their home at the Old Rectory were in the Valency's upper reaches. In one week Hardy's romance with her and the places she introduced him to on their daily rambles, ushered him into a new life: 'She opened the door of the West to me/With its loud sea-lashings,/And cliff-side clashings/Of water rife with revelry'. He declared her in two further poems as the one with whom he aspired 'to walk the world' and later, claimed the place as the key to his life.

Returning home to Dorset with new passion unlocking his writing, he propelled himself towards literary success in order that he could marry her against the wishes of both families. He worked relentlessly, still making a living with architectural jobs and able to visit Cornwall only rarely.

Already introduced to Hardy by my sixth-form readings of *Return of the Native* and *Tess,* I'd been entranced by the slow movements of his characters through landscapes, the connection between 'the road' and the tragic unfolding of lives and stories. So it seemed I had stumbled into a privileged proximity to Hardy here.

Tom told me that Hardy's third novel *A Pair of Blue Eyes,* was set here in the Valency Valley. It was a story with autobiographical echoes about a love affair between the vicar's daughter and a visiting architect from a stonemason's family. He also told me how, after Emma's death in 1912, Hardy returned to the area on a painful pilgrimage. He retraced their steps in the valley and on the high-winged cliffs, as if the paths themselves had been worn by the couple and become a monument to their life together.

Claire Tomalin's biography *Thomas Hardy, The Time-torn Man* reveals the ambiguity of this return: 'Part of him was ecstatically absorbed in recalling Emma and their early love, another part sorrowing for his neglect and unkindness to her'. This remorse and appreciation produced a series of heartbreakingly beautiful poems in which Emma becomes again that spirited young woman on horseback amidst the wild landscape that had once captivated him. Knowing how I often walk at times of stress or gloom or creative stasis, I wonder whether these walks after her death were also an attempt at a cure, as in the words he gives to the newly rejected Stephen in *A Pair of Blue Eyes:* 'Bodily activity will sometimes take the sting out of anxiety as completely as assurance itself.'

Like Hardy, in my first week here, I also fell in love. If for him, this landscape contrasted with his soft Dorset fields, imagine the contrast for me with suburban Surrey. Such a home had already driven me to get a bicycle and launch myself away from concrete on long summer evenings towards the suggestion of soft lanes to ride along on imagined ponies. By the end of my week in Cornwall, Hardy's words rang with my own sentiment: 'The place is pre-eminently ... the region of dream and mystery. The ghostly birds, the pall-like sea, the frothy wind, the eternal soliloquy of the waters ...'

So I return in 2008 with a soft tread, fearful of shattering dreams. I rarely like to return to places that have had a powerful hold on me – perhaps it's a fear of deflation or that things will have changed, but mostly it's a fear of experiencing too keenly a sense of loss for that past time.

As I settle in to the 'Top Town' guesthouse where I stayed in 1976,

I recall the teenager I was, forever on the brink of a blush. I was drawn from my shell into chatter and a restored appetite by the conviviality of hosts and fellow guests brought face to face around a huge dinner table, including Tom, his wife and sister-in-law. Now the place smells of damp and kippers and something deodorised. Apart from mine the rooms are empty and a TV is left talking to itself in the guest lounge. I grow afraid that my adolescent romance can't be sustained, that I'll find Hardy's plots too contrived, his rustic characters painted patronisingly, the landscape here tamed by my last 18 years living in the grand scale of Scottish hills.

I retrace some of my readings – the novels and poetry and biography – and I begin to retrace my physical ways with an updated OS map and a vague sense of my former routes.

As I walk slowly up the Valency Valley, my re-reading of *A Pair of Blue Eyes* starts to take life between the clatter of waterfalls and the tree-lined way. Here, Elfride walked with both her lovers – Stephen Smith the architect, and the older man she rejects him for, Henry Knight. I remember how my younger self related to something in the character of Elfride – her hunger to be loved, her joyous riding of the galloping pony, her restlessness, and an adolescent weakness for tragic poses and melodrama as fate and morality conspired against her.

There's a scene in which her anguish begins to crystallise. As they sit by the waterfall, Knight hails the valley: 'Elfride, I never saw such a sight... The hazels overhang the river's course in a perfect arch, and the floor is beautifully paved. The place reminds me of the passages of a cloister.' Elfride was numbed to Knight's attentions and her beloved waterfall, even to his proposal of marriage that followed shortly; the moment poisoned by the secrets she withholds from him which will ultimately turn this second suitor away from her.

I continue upstream, Minster Wood rising steeply to my right on the other side of the river. Sessile oaks climb the hillside like giant, be-mossed human figures gleaming in partial light, bare arms reaching up in a search, branching just before the canopy into a show of tiny swaying fingers each anxious for light. Beneath them rambles the deep green gloss of holly.

The woodland floor illuminated by this bare light drips green with bluebell leaf, wild garlic, dog's mercury and spears of 'Lords and Ladies'. Flowering celandine carpets the gaps. Every now and again, early jewel-boxes of violet, primrose and pink campion cluster on the banks. The path has been washed clean, but there's a sense of things growing up through silt, of winter being shrugged off and flood damage being overcome. It crackles underfoot with the audible promise of spring.

Emma Gifford wrote recollections of her early courtship with Hardy, which reveal how far *A Pair of Blue Eyes* reflected life: 'Often we walked down the beautiful Valency Valley to Boscastle harbour. We had to jump over stones and climb over a low wall by rough steps, or get through by narrow pathways to come out on great wide spaces suddenly, with a sparkling little brook going the same way, into which we once lost a tiny picnic tumbler, and there it is today, no doubt, between two small boulders.' This incident was immortalised by Hardy in a sketch he made of Emma searching for the tumbler. It also features in his poem, *Under the Waterfall* in which he associates the everyday sensation of his arm in water with searching for the tumbler on that 'fugitive day'; a poem with his characteristic pulse of time and change and loss.

The path climbs through a narrow earthen corridor and then from the subdued light of the woodlands, a kissing gate opens like a window onto a blaze of green field. Crossing it now, the path marked by a dotted line on the map doesn't reveal itself on the ground. I am guided only by a chink in the hedge opposite, by the suggestion of a darker green meandering line teased in the grass by repeated footfall; simply by an instinct as to where the 'desire line', the preferred route of previous walkers, lies.

My early reading of Hardy's novels seem to have drummed the path as custom into my obsessions. When I speculate on the wearing or making of a way; or see the ghost of an old road, disguised now by grass, winding up a hill; or when in East Africa I've passed walkers carrying enormous burdens, then Hardy and his small figures moving in big landscapes are invoked.

In *The Return of the Native* all regular 'haunters' of Egdon Heath are expert path-finders. In the dark on incipient paths, the secret 'lay in the development of the sense of touch in the feet, which comes with years of night rambling in little-trodden spots. To a walker practised in such places a difference between impact on maiden herbage, and on the crippled stalks of a slight footway, is perceptible through the thickest boot or shoe.'

I reach a crossroad. To my left is the Old Rectory, glimpsed in its halo of ragged daffodils – Emma's home, where Hardy stayed as he worked on the church restorations and later returned to visit her. The path to my right drops to the river and then climbs the opposite hillside, traversing eastwards and over a crest to meet the sister church at Lesnewth, which I remember for its extraordinarily tall tower and the cream-coloured stone, mottled mouse-brown. Although I'll continue to St Juliot's, I pause to admire this path that swings across the valley making an ancient connection between places.

In that summer of 1976 the sun scorched down every day, browning lawns and igniting peat on the headland above the harbour so that a fire engine was permanently stationed there pumping water into the earth. I walked from Boscastle one day along higher farmland to the south of 'Emma's' Valley. My intention was to drop to St Juliot's and return to Boscastle alongside the Valency. I remember that somewhere around Lesnewth I got lost. I blundered across fields trying to regain my path and was forced to pass a caravan before climbing over a fence. Stretched out beside the caravan lay a sunbathing man, black-haired and bearded. I whispered past him, afraid to be caught trespassing.

Two evenings later in the Public Bar of the Napoleon Inn to which Tom, Jean and Jo, the grown-up befrienders from my guesthouse had invited me, a gang of locals were singing Cornish folk songs. The sunbather was amongst them. The evening ended on my guesthouse doorstep with him calling me a 'mermaid' and an 'Egyptian maiden' as he stared into my eyes. When I told him that I had slunk past his caravan while he lay sleeping, he said, (and I recorded it in my diary), 'Tis funny how you miss the thing you are most looking for'.

I was plunged into a Hardy novel; had entranced one of his rustic characters. A tragic tale began to take shape in which I was torn between this man who I allowed to kiss my hand and my boyfriend at home, between a life in wild Cornwall or a return to suburbia and school.

As it happened I didn't see him again, but that didn't stop the story. In early memories of that week, the little thrill of this attention came to embody the valley, the village, the experience I had there, and a lost era that I imagined I'd stumbled into. Back home, the magic of the place, my time spent within it, and the jewel-like flirtation ached in me as entirely inseparable losses.

The tower of St Juliot's rises from the north-facing slope, leading me forward along field edges and over stiles. Seen from below it seems curiously high and prominent but I know that approached from the higher road to its northwest, it appears low and tucked away, a deliberate strategy to conceal the churches in this valley from seafaring raiders. Hardy first approached the church from a different direction. Yet, as it was the tower that brought him here to make drawings for its restoration, in one sense it stood iconic on his horizon all the way from Dorset and perhaps even as he looked back over his shoulder on his journey home.

I know from reading Tomalin's biography how starting school in Dorchester at the age of ten meant a daily walk for Hardy of three miles each way. He observed hares, and 'learnt to read the noises of the fields and the woods, the bark of the fox'. This time for solitude and reflection perhaps fostered his keen observations of nature. But as Tomalin says, 'Walking the roads, meeting others on the road, exchanging news with travellers, being overtaken by riders, carts and carriers or offered lifts', will also have educated him about human life and led towards speculation and then drama, exercising his imagination and walking him towards his writerly sensibility.

When I'm leading 'walking and writing' workshops, I'll often ask participants to summon a character into their heads, perhaps with the aid of a picture. Before they set their character in motion I ask them to consider a few things including what the character has on their feet, why they're in this place and what they carry in their pockets: a clue to hidden lives, hidden purposes. Then they walk, making observations through the filter of the character's emotions and motivations. Asking 'what if?' of a character when engaging with a place through the senses is the kind of 'play' that makes storytellers of us all. I like to think of ten-year old Thomas Hardy playing such a game as he walked to and from school.

I climb the stile between field and sloping churchyard, passing the first wheel-headed cross, and finding alleys of daffodil-blown softness between crooked headstones carved with the repeated family name, Jose. The heavy-looking church door with its huge keyhole purrs open at my touch, stepping me onto grey stone, paled by subdued light. A sign reassures me that the brass has already been stolen but that the church is left open for my 'enjoyment, rest, and spiritual re-creation.' I love the double meaning of 'spiritual re-creation'– as if the human soul is a building, a church tower to be restored, re-created. But it also suggests exercise of the soul as in a run or cycle ride. It seems to me that if the visitor has been 'present in the moment' to observe, enquire and imagine as she walks up the valley, then some spiritual recreation will have happened.

There's an unspoken acknowledgment in the church that of the many pilgrims who have arrived at it, few nowadays are on a religious mission. This pilgrim, for example, is drawn to Hardy's sketches of the pew ends; to the plaques commemorating Emma designed and commissioned by her husband in 1913. There's a window that I don't remember engraved with images and lines from the poems. It includes 'their' waterfall, and his journey to Lyonesse depicted on a path meandering over rounded west country hills. A cliff top on which a girl sits on a pony, hair streaming behind her, inevitably evokes (with a small shiver as I read it) the lines from his poem *Beeny Cliff*: 'O the opal and the sapphire of that wandering western sea,/ And the woman riding high above with bright hair flapping free - / The woman who I loved so, and who loyally loved me.'

His memories of their time in the valley tinkle with water and a sense of sunken enclosure. But he more often conflates Emma's spirit with the wild beauty of the cliff landscape to the north. The contrast, as one climbs from damp leaf-filled valleys onto the shaly exposure and vertiginous drops of the highest cliffs in England (if you consider Cornwall to be in England), characterises this place and seems to generate and deepen for me the human drama of *A Pair of Blue Eyes.*

In the poem *If You Had Known*, Hardy describes a wet walk back from Beeny Cliff towards the Old Rectory 'by crooked ways and over stiles of stone'. Stiles and gateposts of slate here seem silk-edged with the wear of hands and feet and weather. The distinctive 'curzy-way' dry stone walls with slates diagonally arranged are lichen-mottled like tweed, decorated with celandine leaves and cushions of stonecrop. Hardy's 'crooked ways' seem to me characteristic of the scale of North Cornwall with its tight valleys, intimate fields, and the lanes that tunnel deep below the bordering farmland.

Sumptuous growth over built structures means that walls, corners, culverts, channels, paths, become softened by earth, disguised by ivy, fashioned into emerald mysteries. The scale means that even a 17 year old cannot be bored by walking here. A few strides brings a change in view; a small climb reveals the next valley; a dropped hedge reveals the sea. Walking unlocks the treasures of this valley.

I also explored the cliffs to the east and west of Boscastle in 1976 as I walked in increasing circles and offshoots from my centre – circles which moved me towards orientation, recognition, familiarity and finally a sense of 'owning' the place, or perhaps it owning me. This walking ritual, a sort of 'beating of the bounds', that I learnt here is now instinctive when I visit new places, a link perhaps to Hardy who walked his way to a native knowledge of London in the five years that he lived there.

The summer after my first visit, I returned with The Boyfriend, the one who had been much missed but also dismissed in fits of anger or independence the previous year. The diary I kept on the 1977 holiday reveals the miles I marched him, seeking out and showing off 'my' places, though we also extended our walks to new destinations. We would do a long day-walk from the campsite and then in the evening tramp four miles to Boscastle along the cliffs to go to the pub. I don't remember if he complained.

On this return I've walked the cliffs too. I climbed onto Beeny in spring sunshine and a rib-slicing north-east wind, panting through the progressions in height – Buckator, Rusey and finally onto the windblown wasteland, High Cliff, where mushroom-shaped islands of turf cling to bare rock. I crouched amongst tussocks for the view across to Lundy Island; to Cambeak north of me, before the turn of the coast to Crackington Haven. I gazed back west to Boscastle harbour, and beyond to the white look-out tower on Willapark and the cliffs stretching away to Tintagel Head. Below me yawned a vertical black cliff, the face I could see scarred with seams of blood-coloured stone and white quartz. Distantly, far below, I heard the crack of breakers, and saw the sea mustering cloudy-grey onto the shore after several recent storm-days.

Emma was invoked in lines from *I Found Her Out There*, 'Where the ocean breaks / On the purple strand, / And the hurricane shakes /

The solid land.' And so was Elfride, Emma's fictional alter-ego, leading both her lovers at different times onto a perilous ledge. 'There far beneath and before them, lay the everlasting stretch of ocean; there, upon detached rocks, were the white screaming gulls, seeming ever intending to settle, and yet always passing on. Right and left ranked the toothed and zigzag line of storm-torn heights...'

Hardy's dialogue between landscape and character, human mood and nature, had captured me as a reader by 1976, and has coloured my own fiction writing. Almost unconsciously, I conjure characters out of particular places, or observe places and landscapes through the state of mind or qualities of my characters. When Henry Knight dangles from the edge of the cliff by two handfuls of heather in one of the most dramatic moments of *A Pair of Blue Eyes,* he observes: 'We colour according to our moods the objects we survey. The sea would have been a deep neutral blue, had happier auspices attended the gazer: it was now no other than distinctly black to his vision. That narrow white border was foam, he knew well; but its boisterous tosses were so distant as to appear a pulsation only, and its plashing was barely audible. A white border to a black sea – his funeral pall and its edging.'

I leave the two-dimensional version of Beeny Cliff etched onto St Juliot's window, close the church door behind me and return down the valley, appreciating the change in perspective as the sea is caught between diagonal slopes. Sinking back into the sub-marine, moss-drenched world below Newmills, I cross the river and start to climb steeply up through Peter's Wood. The path follows a tributary of the Valency, levelling out as it approaches the back gate of Minster churchyard. Just before I go in, something low against the dark bank catches my eye. A small grey headstone is inscribed with the pagan symbol of a full moon, a crescent resting its back against each side. Below it I read:

'JOAN WYTTE
BORN 1775
DIED 1813

IN BODMIN GAOL
BURIED 1998
NO LONGER ABUSED.'

This was the 'fighting fairy woman of Bodmin' – seer, diviner and healer; user of holy wells and cloutie trees. She was imprisoned for GBH after a tooth abscess made her bad tempered. Her coffin was connected with poltergeist activities and remained unburied. Later it was acquired by the Boscastle witchcraft museum and given a proper burial here.

It makes me think of Emma, referring in her recollections to witchcraft still being practised amongst the 'primitive inhabitants' here and also of Hardy's stories in which sympathetic magic is an integral part of rural custom. As he says in *The Return of the Native,* 'the impulses of all such outlandish hamlets are pagan still'.

I step inside Minster church where a book records the handwritten prayers of visitors. Its subjects are the terminally ill, soldiers away at war, the love-lost and bereaved. It strikes me how these prayers – written in ink that will fade, on paper that will dampen and decay – are not unlike the charms of rotting cloth in the Rocky Valley a little southwest of here, dangling in the salt winds from a cloutie tree.

Of the three churches in this valley, Minster feels the deepest sunk into a hollow, its tower almost appearing to touch the moist steep bank of spent daffodil and wild garlic. Inlaid with words of love and loss, the churchyard recalls me to Hardy's 'ghost-walks' when he returned here after Emma's death, back to find the girl he knew before 38 years of marriage dulled his appreciation of her. *In The Phantom Horsewoman,* he is the man who 'comes and stands / in a careworn craze, / And looks at the sands / And the seaward haze...' and 'what his back years bring / - A phantom of his own figuring', 'a ghost-girl rider'. In *The Haunter,* a ghost follows him that he doesn't see, telling us, 'Yes, / I companion him to places / Only dreamers know, / Where the shy hares print long paces, / Where the night rooks go'.

Referring to these poems of repressed sorrow and forgotten love,

Tomalin compares him to 'an archaeologist uncovering objects that have not been seen for many decades, bringing them out into the light, examining them, some small pieces, some curious bones and broken bits, and some shining treasures.' It's almost as if in this place where, 'lonely I found her,/ The sea birds around her,' the essence of Emma, the cackle of wind and gulls is all waiting to be rediscovered. In revisiting his passion for Emma and her valley in footsteps and words, he must have faced a personal and creative challenge.

In 1976 I often walked the hill between the harbour and 'Top-Town' – down to swim in the evenings, and back up to my guesthouse. Higher up the hill from the guesthouse was the studio of artist Carole Vincent, who was coaching me in drawing and painting each morning as preparation for A-level Art, and for a portfolio I needed for art college entry. Palpable in my diary scribblings, amongst anxieties about letters not received or protestations of independence from The Boyfriend, is the excitement I felt in the creative focus on my drawing and painting tasks each morning.

Every lunchtime, a group of us sat in the sunny garden with hunks of Carole's oven-warm bread and glasses of homemade beer. I revelled in finding myself treated as an adult at the studio, as well as in the guesthouse and the pub. I enjoyed the chat. But equally I seemed to need a daily dose of solitude. After lunch I would leave with my map to find a new walk. This pattern is one I still follow on days I shape for creative work.

I climb the hill through the village slowly now, winding between squat white cottages with bright paintwork, low slate roofs and crooked chimneys. Geraniums and palm trees throng the gardens. I pass the Napoleon Inn and find my way back to Carole Vincent's house and studio. I guess she's still here from the colourful concrete sculptures that add oases of colour in the garden. I find her at the sink in her studio; the same woman. She came here for a six month teaching contract and remains in the same house 47 years later. I feel a keen sense of joy in this fragment of permanence. She's still teaching, encouraging other artists, developing her own work, swimming. She tells me she makes beer to the same 1976 recipe. But this time we drink sherry.

Carole takes me up to the first floor where her father's restored writing desk stands. It's made of pale oak inlaid with leather, and is bare of clutter. There's no sign of a computer. She invites me to sit at the desk. Drawers slink open to reveal neat lines of pens and notebooks, plain white pages inscribed with a sloping black script that I remember from her early publicity materials. I spread my hands on the desk and look down through the familiar tumble of cottages in the Jordan valley. The sea opens beyond the harbour, and I look out towards the horizon.

A door opened for me when I was here first, and I see now a clear pathway between that 17 year old who was learning to draw and paint and the woman who writes in 2008. We are not so different. I've not outgrown the romance that helped me 'find my feet' and shaped my passion for paths and for walking as well as for literature.

Would I ever get any writing done at Carole's desk, I wonder? But then, I know now that if a place takes hold of you, and you simply ask, 'What if?', it isn't long before a story presents itself.

Dancing, kicking up her legs

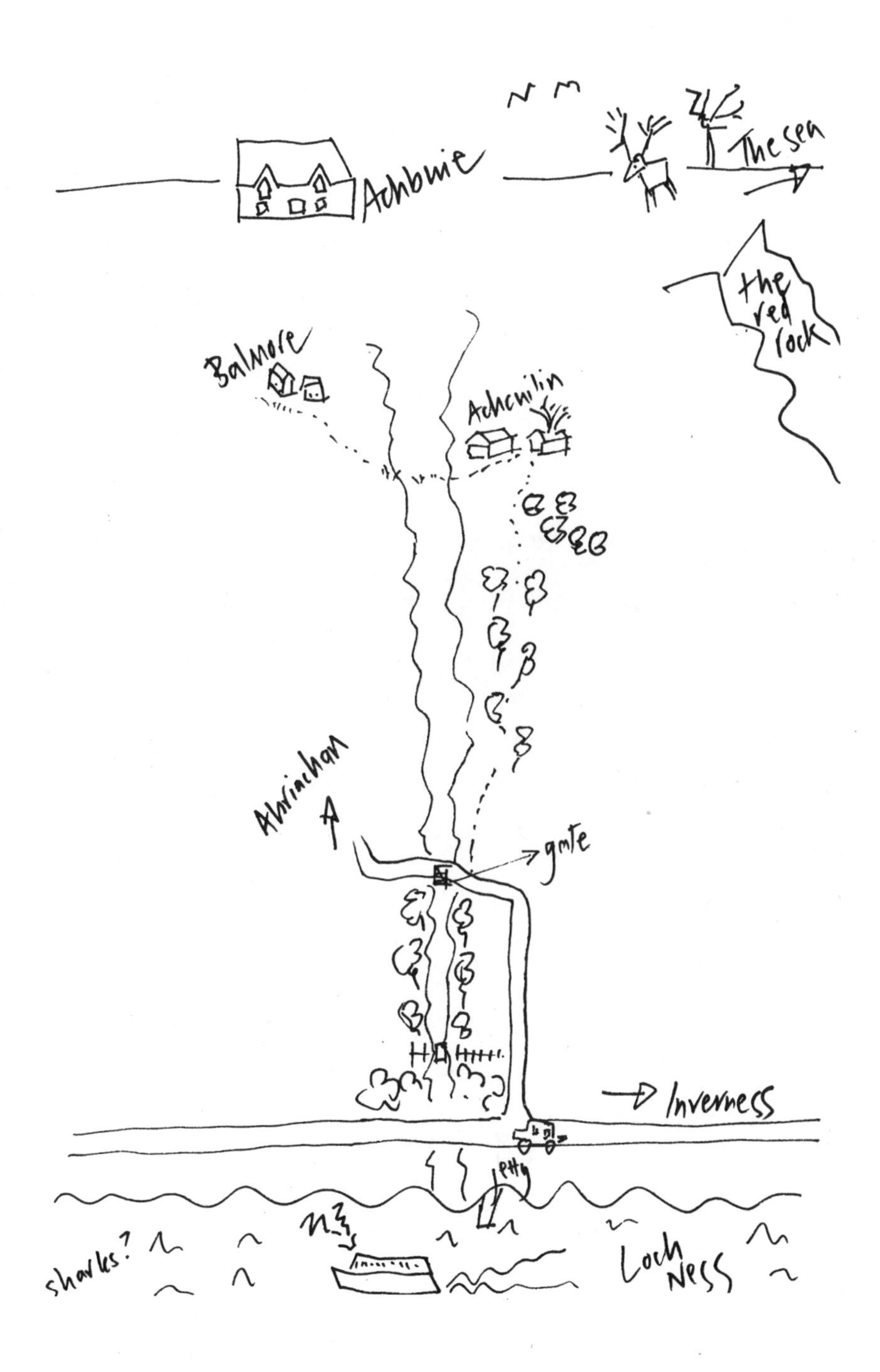
Achbuie
The sea
the red rock
Balmore
Achcuilin
Abriachan
gate
Inverness
jetty
sharks?
Loch Ness

A hillside near Abriachan, Loch Ness

Spring there is more than colour; it is music and scent. The burns literally hum down the hillside, the trees have rhythm in their shaking.

> Ness MacDonald, 'Country Dweller's Year', *Scots Magazine, April 1946*

Despite late April sunshine, spring was still holding its breath when I arrived on 'her' hillside. I was a thousand feet up at Abriachan, where a dormer-windowed house straddles lush pastureland below and the scratch of heather on the open moor above. This is Achbuie where at the age of nineteen, writer Jessie Kesson (1916-1994) came after a year of virtual imprisonment in a mental hospital. She was 'boarded out', as the practice was known, living with and helping an elderly woman on her croft. Amongst the smell of bracken-mould and primroses, on a hill so high and steep that, as she said, 'you feel any moment you might topple into Loch Ness below', she rambled freely for the six months or so that she stayed. The visceral thrill of the place in springtime pulses through her writing in different genres ever after.

It was curiosity about this powerful influence that took me there in early spring. I wanted to share her exuberance and find the Red Rock she wrote about. And there, high on the moor to the north-east of Achbuie, seen through my wind-tugged hair – a slash of steep gully sliced inland from the Loch into a south-facing cliff. Red and crumbly, fissured in long downward strikes, a superb visual play was created by the orange-red of newly exposed rock against the petrol-glazed blue of age. I knew from Isobel Murray's biography *Writing her Life* that as Jessie ran and rambled across the hillside here she was followed by a stream of younger girls intrigued by her supposed 'experience'. With its precipitous pathways of loose rock, I could see the lure for a gaggle of youngsters. This was at the far reaches of Abriachan, at the door to another world, edgy and dangerous and out of sight of the cottage and a watching old lady.

Rites of passage were played out here according to Jessie's writing – a childish game came close to an early sexual adventure. Later, her courtship with her future husband, John Kesson, who quarried the red sand rock, involved meetings on Sunday afternoons. Lying in the shadow of the red rock, they used 'The Book', which she was required to carry on the Sabbath, as a pillow.

That day in late April I climbed above the red rock to where the open moor levels. The wind carved down the lochside, and the bare birches rang maroon against a clear sky. Deer poured uphill on winter-dusky heather whose wiry stems snapped at my bootlaces. I kept turning, wondering whose step it was that caught at the back of mine, half expecting to find a line of children in a giggling retreat.

Before dropping towards Caiplich I savoured the long views that Jessie wrote of in *I to the Hills* through the eyes of a character called Chris: 'High up in the shadow of the Red Rock, she would lie, knowing that never in a lifetime could she absorb the changing moods and varying beauty of the vista unfolded below her.' I gazed southwards towards Fort Augustus and the steep-sided finale of the Loch. On its east side, beyond water-pocketed escarpments, the Cairngorms displayed long low-reaching fingers of late snow. To the north-east, the Moray Firth and the sea's horizon sparkled, the lure that perhaps took the young Jessie away to Inverness, next returning to Abriachan for her honeymoon, and repeatedly afterwards in words.

Up on the open moor, the curlew burbled its high lilt. Peewits crashed within a whisper of the earth as they performed their jitterbug aerobatic displays. The notes they beat in the air with their broad wings seemed reassuring heralds of the spring. 'Soon, soon', they soothed.

I was curious about this hillside for another reason.

When I was first writing short stories, and about ten years before I came across Jessie Kesson's work, I wrote *Keeping Away from the Water.* A young woman is returning to the area of her childhood home, above Loch Ness at Abriachan, and the visit provokes keen memories of growing up on this hillside playground, and of the loss of her father. I wrote about the child's experience of the place as if it was animate: 'Voices burble up with the Spring wind, with the sunshine, in the birch trees. I hear them best if I lay my head in the whipping grasses and close my eyes. They never quite let me hear them directly - who they are, what they're saying. I crunch down on last year's bracken by the burn, finding primroses amongst the rusty deadness, turning their pale faces to be licked by the sun.'

I'm surprised now that I set my story in a place that I'd only glimpsed at then, in passing. Perhaps it was reading Eona Macnicol's *The Small Herdsman,* that prompted it. A native of Abriachan, similar themes find their place in her story. The memory of a terrifying childhood emerges against the backdrop of, '...pasture and bracken and trees, and the hyacinthine Loch glinting between them'. My story was personalised by memories of immersion in the wilder corners of my own childhood garden but when I re-read it now I feel a chime with Jessie Kesson's hillside – the drop to the loch, the animation, music and spirit world of spring, and with her themes of childhood pain and loss. But it wasn't until 2006 that I properly explored her work.

Commissioned by BBC Radio 4 to choose and dramatise a short story by a twentieth century woman writer, I beat a trail through my favourites from Katherine Mansfield, to Helen Simpson and Alice

Munro, but it wasn't until I stumbled upon Jessie's *Until Such Times* that the project took off. It's the tale of a young girl sent to live with her grandmother and envious Invalid Aunt, while her single mother (referred to as another aunt) searches for suitable circumstances to give her a decent home. The child waits, painfully, for the 'until such times' of the title. The story evokes the inner world of a lonely child who finds solace in woodland nature and the moments of her beloved grandmother's full attention. The story's conclusion suggests murderous triumph over the Invalid Aunt, making the story inherently dramatic, but it was something else which made it compelling for me.

I sought out her other writing, discovered more of the fictionalised re-workings of her own traumatic childhood years. The dull bass beat of pain was always there, but was somehow overlain with bright, poetic joys found in nature or brief moments of love and belonging. I began to realise that it was the intensity of the inner life of troubled children that I connected to. I wasn't traumatised as a child but I was introverted, the inner world I inhabited keenly alive, and I've come to think of it as the dark inkwell from which my pen flows.

Jessie Kesson's childhood is described by her biographer Isobel Murray as 'a series of violent shifts of surroundings and circumstances, with no ongoing family support to provide stability or continuity.' She was born illegitimate and lived in Elgin slums with her mother who recited nineteenth century poetry and shared her extensive knowledge as they walked barefoot through the countryside. Her mother was also a drinker and a small time prostitute and Jessie was eventually taken away from her to live in an orphanage. Unable to continue her education despite excellence at school, she took on various unsatisfactory jobs, performing poorly because she was enticed away by the outdoors, or lost in a book of poetry while the ironing scorched. At the age of eighteen she spent a year in Aberdeen Royal Mental Hospital following an attack on the matron of the girls' hostel who had implied a slur on her mother.

Despite such early experiences she became famous in her lifetime, with two novels becoming feature films, including *Another Time,*

Another Place. But it was writing for radio in which she was most prolific and successful. Ironically it was success in this medium – ephemeral, unarchived, largely unpublished – that now, unjustly, might allow her work to fade.

Thankfully the text of her short radio play, *The Childhood*, set at Abriachan, has been collected in *Somewhere Beyond*. Danny Kernon, a young lad removed from his alcoholic mother in Glasgow, to be boarded-out with an 'aunt' on this same hillside, is shocked by the sudden change of environment: 'I had never seen a hill before. Nor have I seen one more terrible. It rose sheerly out of the Loch. It was full of deep, narrow gulleys, and covered with great rocks.' The other boarded-out Glasgow youngsters, having had more time to adjust to the landscape, only increase his terror, goading: 'The Loch hasna got a bottom... You jump it, Kernon... just one wee slip! He's yella!' The play thrums with Danny's deep ache for his mother. Jessie Kesson evokes the emotional fragility of boarded-out children who had to laugh in whispers and never once knew '...what it was to be able to put their heads on the 'aunt's' lap and sob out the bewildering hurts of childhood'

In time Danny stands up to the other boys, drawing strength out of his solitude, from song, and his intimate knowledge of the hill and the hundreds of burns that leap down it. '...I could have counted the flowers that grew on the hill by the Loch. I knew each stone. My hands became scarred with grasping the bracken. I discovered that the primrose cheats the eye: only its flower was softer than velvet, sweeter than any mortal things. Its leaves were rough and hairy and ugly.'

On my second visit I'm startled after only a ten-day absence by the progress of spring. It's a day of sudden warmth and this time I take the sunny green slopes below Achbuie rather than the moor bristling above. The valley sweeps down between two rises. On one sits the most southerly cottage of the village at Balmore. The spur under the moor opposite holds the ruined crofts of Achculin. A burn begins its run to the Loch between them, shadowed on each side lower down by birches.

The cropped greenness of the pasture and its angle invites me to run in Julie-Andrews-gladness; a child again. It's here that I imagine Jessie making her own plunge to the Lochside in a joyful errand to meet the van that couldn't get up the steep road, the van that was the grocer, butcher, and draper combined, to which she carried eggs in return for 'the messages'. I imagine her, with her ear for the music and rhythm of song and speech, singing and laying her feet to a tune as she went. Perhaps it would be like the dance music heard by Isabel in *Where the Apple Ripens,* 'following her all the way to Corbie's wood, and echoing through her mind long after she had reached home. Dispelling sleep itself.

'And you shall drink freely
The dews of Glensheerie
That stream in the starlight' .'

Or perhaps she would be arguing with a shower as she hurried downhill:

'Rainie Rainie Rattlestanes
Dinna rain on me
Rain on Johnnie Groat's house
Far across the sea.'

I sit on damp grass near Balmore. Birdsong bubbles in a galaxy around my head. Long buzzard-mewls stretch high notes above me against the lighter, closer, chips, trills and warbles of stonechats, skylarks, meadow pipits. The passing buzz of a bee. An aeroplane drones from one side of the loch to the other, its hum eclipsed behind the rocky knoll above Achbuie. Then a crack of sound springs my eyes open as a jet banks behind my shoulder, tilts low over the Loch. It's as if spring has lofted everything sky-wards.

Soft unexplained pops rise from the grass. A palm rested on a tender nettle tingles sweetly. On this north-facing slope, bracken heads have broken through the turf, heads still curled tight. They look strong and fleshy on their thick single stems, but innocent, belying their summer rampancy. Bracken, as Jessie pointed out, is called in Gaelic, 'the lovely curse'. Few plants can compete with it, fending off predators, as it does, with an arsenal of chemical weapons including cyanide.

John McCarthy described the marvel of 'walking into a cathedral of light in Oxfordshire,' after his release from five years of captivity in Lebanon. And I imagine Jessie Kesson stepping from the deadened enclosure and stale air of the mental hospital into this cacophony of sound and the sense of elevation. Coming from a regimented institution with every thought and activity crowded by other lives, this could hardly have failed to provoke her free spirit and to animate her feet in exploration. Perhaps it recalled her to those barefoot walks with her mother and a sense of inhabiting again her wild self.

I'm pulled to my feet and into the valley to cross the burn, and up the other side onto south-facing Achculin where bracken has been sunned higher from the earth, now tall enough to brush my calves. Colour hums against colour – slate blue of hyacinth and Loch, lettuce-green of young bracken against the pink granite walls. The rusty corrugated iron roofs have been weighted with rocks except for one, burst off by the spraying branches of a rowan tree. Above the buildings is a steep rock outcrop. Below, the spur of hill runs towards the Loch, decorated with brilliant buttons of gorse bush or 'whin'. In Gaelic the name for gorse comes from the word for 'wrangle' or 'quarrel' and like a brassy blonde wearing gold jewellery she's here in a tussle with those around her, draining colour from the exuberant birch leaves, the Loch below and the bluebells. But perhaps you're allowed to be a bit showy in spring.

'The smell of Spring in the hills is a blending of peaty thickness, bracken-mould, flowers' spicyness, and clean, quick, purge of the wind' Jessie wrote in the *Scots Magazine*, and her scents are all here. It's the gorse that beguiles me to stop with its coconut-scented panting. Along with the heat, it licks the hillside promiscuous. Violets on the slope have opened their limbs wide to the sun to reveal their dark, secret clefts.

Sure of Jessie's route down the burn, I follow a fence tented by a crisp brown cover of last year's bracken. Down I go, into the shade of coppiced hazel woods where I lose the bold skyline of the steep lochsides. Without the gaudy whins, my eyes slowly adjust to wood anemones glimmering as pale stars on the ground and the green rise of bluebell tips.

I hear the burn chittering on my right as I tumble out onto the steep tarmac lane that climbs to Abriachan from the Loch. It's breezeless and shaded. I cross the burn, follow the lane a little south, wondering where Jessie would have found the next part of her descent. And there, between one burn and the next is a gate and a path marked by a scattered line of brown leaves, leading down between trees. It is unremarked on the map and delights me with the soft secrecy of its way. Here there is soprano birch leaf and the bronzy tenor of the first clusters of oak leaves. Lit from behind, caught by breezes, they jig against the dark interlocking antlers of the branches. Blaeberry bushes burst around my feet, already belled with round red flowers.

The burns on each side of me chant louder or softer according to the windings of the path between them. I walk slowly for fear of missing something. The Lochside clamour starts to penetrate the woodland. Motorbikes have been sprung from winter garages to roar along the A82. A voice so amplified it's inaudible rises through the trees and I glimpse the white wake pulled behind a tourist boat. Would Jessie have been running at this point towards the grocer's van, despite the eggs she holds?

The sense of a well-loved, shared path keeps pulling me Loch-wards, until it leads to a wicket gate in an unyielding high fence. Beyond it I see the purple flash of rhododendron, hints of laid paths, ponds and house roofs. I skirt the fence to the southerly burn, looking for another way, smashing through bramble and brush and over fallen logs. My legs are scratched and bloody, torn by the open edges of dead bracken stem. With soil and moss smearing my hands, I'm returned to my childhood garden, my wilderness of rust-glazed water and bracken. Hints of suburbia hang between birch branches and drone with the distant lawnmower.

Then I'm out onto the A82, shuddered by the wind-suck of juggernaut, bike, van. I cross, and retreat from the road to the pink shingle shore onto which vast waters splash. A heavy afternoon sky brings a few drops of rain from the south. The Loch sucks at the shore. It's capricious – glittering blue when seen from one direction, then lashing in black and white troughs, monster-deep and dark from another.

I think of Kesson's descriptions of walking to church along this shore, but having to stick to the road on a Sunday rather than 'scushing through the soft, white sand by the lochside,' laughing and talking with those of her own age once they were far enough ahead of the adults. This rattling chatter seemed to mark her time here too, despite 'her sense of being an outsider wherever she went, an 'ootlin' as she called it, marching to a different beat from other people.' I like this Scots word 'ootlin' – the territory of the writer perhaps. As a shy child, I always felt on the edge, peering in, choosing friends who were also outsiders, alienated by obesity, religion or other kinds of oddness.

My mother's attempts to integrate me with other children by enrolling me at Brownies or in a summer holiday club at the local park both ended before they began – with her driving me away again, crying. I retreated to my garden refuge where there were acorns to gather and serve to my dolls at mealtimes, or I could dig for treasures and inhabit my own world.

Even before her year in mental hospital, when she was staying at the girls' hostel in Aberdeen, Jessie wrote of an association between spring and rebellion: 'It was only when I began to "break a rule" that the girls began to accept me and confided in me. But I didn't break the rule for that reason. It was broken for no reason that I can give words to. I'd smelt the spring. A different thing altogether from knowing it was there. I smelt it almost before it came, as if it had told me it was coming.'

When she walked on this edge of land and water at the age of nineteen she was perhaps already becoming comfortable with the rebellious identity that would free her from unpromising beginnings and define her as a writer, bringing an intensity of self-awareness, a love of nature, a humour and spirit that overcame adversity. I like to think it was an extreme change of environment and the experience of spring here that propelled her into that self.

After six months, the sensuality and physicality of the place became overwhelming and she ran away.

Despite this, it's clear that the hillside at Abriachan remained special. She chose it for her honeymoon. She chose it as the place where her ashes were to be scattered; a hillside so alive to her that she returned to it again and again in her writing. Perhaps from the rootlessness of her childhood years she found some stillness or sense of security here in proximity to nature. Perhaps it was for her as it was for Danny in *The Childhood* who drew strength from the permanence of what he found in the country, saying, 'I was safe with all those things undying'.

As I turn away from the Loch and begin the climb back, I feel that today I've brushed shoulders with a character who, by her own admission, was like a 'tornado' at nineteen when she whirled into the life of the old lady at Achbuie making her ask, 'is there no settle in you?' Alastair Scott described her much later in her life as a 'one-woman riot' and Isobel Murray's biography suggests she stayed that way until her death. Quite apart from the sweet pain and joy of her stories, she's bequeathed to me a spring day in her special place. I've feasted my senses.

With limbs swinging I laugh and pant, sweating up through the green song-tunnels beside the burn. Jessie's granddaughter described how her grandmother would be remembered – 'Dancing, kicking up her legs' – and it seems an apt description also for this hillside in springtime.

Ways of Life

Château de Lavigny, Switzerland, August 2012

The weather has changed. Cool air and rain keep us writing indoors rather than on the balcony that overlooks the cobbled courtyard, or under the shade of the plane tree. The five of us here are like shadows to each other during the day – footsteps in the corridor below, a door closing, and occasional face to face negotiations at the fridge.

There are other writers to negotiate as we move around. My room is named 'Nabokov', who was a regular visitor here and near neighbour in Montreux. Other doors invoke other legends: 'Hemingway', 'Camus', 'Faulkner', all writers at one time published by Ledig-Rowohlt, who owned the Château and was described by Christina Foyle as, 'crazy, wild and full of panache'. His wife, Jane, bequeathed their home to be used as a 'Writers' Colony' in his memory in 1996. Words teem from shelves of books left by visiting writers from around the world over successive summers, alongside silk wallpapers, Picasso ceramics and other treasures recalling literary friendships such as watercolours by Henry Miller and letters from John Updike.

It would be easy to be intimidated by these literary ghosts filling the high-ceilinged rooms with their scribbling. But there's good will in their legacy, the continuing spirit of internationalism, creativity and friendship that keeps us focussed and brings us around a table with food and wine in the evenings: India, Nigeria, USA, Denmark, Britain.

As I write, debates inspired by the 'Edinburgh World Writers' Conference', commemorating a similar event 50 years earlier, rumble on. 'Is a novelist a literary activist?' 'Should Literature be political?' These are questions addressed by Egyptian writer, Ahdaf Soueif. Like her I don't like the word 'should' anywhere near art. But as she says, writers are also citizens and are at work as the Arab Spring takes its course.

In connecting us to the lives of others, literature can be a profound means of furthering change in the world. As Soueif says: 'A work of fiction lives by empathy – the extending of my self into another's, the willingness to imagine myself in someone else's shoes. This itself is a political act: empathy is at the heart of much revolutionary action.' But should writers be marching – or at least writing – in action at the moment of crisis rather than shutting themselves away to mature current world realities into fiction?

I don't take the map on my morning walks any longer; I've learnt my one-hour radius and stay within it, walking almost as I do at home, without making decisions, just seeing what each junction decides and greeting the dog-walkers along the way. There's still an element of exploring as I join up the paths I know, experiment with the route so I can miss out a section on a road, or cut out some up and down by going through a vineyard. I take delight in my ability to improvise.

If I'm tempted beyond my radius, to see where that sweet-looking path goes, or in a digression along the Arboretum, I tell myself that it will cost me writing time. Those forays are for a longer walk, or more usually for the bicycle rides I take in the evening, after which I return panting with exhilaration and effort from riding up the hill behind us or down to the Lake. Perhaps with this pattern of activity I'm agreeing with Ralph Waldo Emerson when he said: 'In the morning a man walks with his whole body; in the evening, only with his legs.'

Paths pull at me. They course through my early memories. When I was seven, a sloping swathe cut by repeated footfall through an Alpine flower meadow took me at a run between chalet and lakeshore to swim. Visualising that trampled line now unlocks the entire Austrian holiday. A line of moonlit stones in *Hansel and Gretel*; Little Red Riding Hood's mysterious ways through the dark forest; they drew me into the story.

I stumbled upon southeastern Spain's Mozarabic Trails when walking there in the 1990s and was lured back by their miraculous utility, their carefully engineered ways through plunging mountain terrain. The antiquity of the paths and their origins intrigued me; the context of their building, and even their naming. And so I wandered off the physical path into the history of Al-Andalus and the relationships between different religious communities that have become so much more pertinent in the years since.

With so many old ways lost as functional routes because of newer forms of transport, a search for those that remain alive for the pedestrian criss-crossing of people's lives, news, business took me on the second walk in this section – a village walk in Kenya.

By walking these paths in Spain and Kenya, I hoped to understand something of the places they connect and pass through, and the people who walk or walked them. They both kick up issues of tolerance and humanity along with dust and pebbles. Walking 'in someone else's shoes' (or without shoes if they are) and on their paths connects one to their stories and rouses the imagination. An open mind accompanying a good walk might just increase our ability to empathise and cross boundaries in a complex world and make for better participants in the 'human race'.

Stairway to Heaven?

Vall de Laguart
Campell
Benimaurell
Fleix
caballo verde
Collado de Gargas
pencil case
Castell de castells
Bolulla castle
Beniarda
Guadalest
Bolulla
Callosa d'En Sarria
FINISH
Paso de los contadores
Sella
Relleu
START
Benidorm

Relleu to Valle de Laguart
La Marina Alta y Baja,
Alicante, Spain

Walking – cuts a line through 21st century life.

Hamish Fulton, from *Seven Short Walks,* 2005, Fundación Cesar Manrique, Lanzarote

On the brink of a ravine just below the village of Fleix, cautions are muttered in my ear. I snatch glimpses of the path that winds down a 240 metre drop. Way below I can see that it loops in relaxed arcs, but only after ten tight, twisting relays of stairs. And before that, it will have to cross the Barranco de Salt, invisible from here. It's clear that these paths bond the natural and the man-made. Their lines below me are artful, an intriguing adaptation to the terrain in this great vault of gaping land between mountain ranges. I wonder, though, if they're in good enough condition to carry me safely after so many centuries?

My side of the gorge is shivering in morning shadow, but on the wall opposite, where I can see my path's partner zig-zagging up, winter sun flares on bursts of crimson foliage amongst the cactuses. A screen of shade has been rolled down to illuminate bleach-white boulders in the dry riverbed. The gorge is shocked in half; holds within it two very different territories. I've stared for so long that it begins to seem I'm looking up, rather than down. I'm staring into the vaulted ceiling of a cathedral, and admiring the perfect meeting of its ribs; a grand space dedicated to symmetry, pattern and strength; an evocation perhaps of Heaven on Earth.

Yesterday, my first view of Valle de Laguart from the pass, Collada de Gargas, had struck me as fearful and unforgiving. Grey and austere, spurs leading off the Sierras of Carrasca and Mediodia were scarred with parallel lines that highlighted their monstrous, rolling forms. Ravine led off ravine. I had brief glimpses of pendulous pathways below that shivered with lack of sunlight. The cavernous depths and high-rise buttresses unsettled me as I descended the sloping valley through three villages of Bennimaurell, Fleix, and Campell that sit just proud of the great canyon edge, surrounded by the extensive cherry orchards whose fruits are famed across European markets. Above these villages runs the Caballo Verde ridge, where the last Morisco rebels tried to withstand expulsion from Spain in 1609 and were either killed by Royal troops or forced into exile from nearby ports.

I plan to traverse east to west along the Valle de Laguart by crossing to its northern side and then re-crossing ravines, or *barrancos*, at three points. In this way I'll take three pairs of 'Mozarabic Trails' today, plummeting and climbing perversely in and out of the gorges, to make an ascent of over 900 metres. I've been warned about accidents in this place, am wary of the cavern opening beneath my feet. I wait on the brink, willing the sunlight to dress my side of the canyon with more of a welcome.

The Valle de Laguart in the mountain ranges of La Marina in south-eastern Spain has been coined '*la catedral de senderismo*' – the cathedral of walking. I first came across a Mozarabic Trail here when walking about ten years ago, and was taken by its ingenuity and precipitousness. But it was getting dark and we were lost so there was no time to explore it further.

I began to plan a week's continuous walk through La Marina that would bring me to Valle de Laguart. Before leaving home, I bruised my knees on a hard floor, wrangling with four 1:50,000 military maps to conjure solid ground out of their abstractions. The contours were so crammed against each other, it was hard to interpret what was up and what down. One thing the maps did make clear was that the faintly drawn Mozarabic Trails make direct cross-country lines whereas the roads loop and curl to find high ground and sedate inclines. When I began to explore the word 'Mozarab' in advance of my trip and to research the origins of the paths, a complex story began to emerge which drew me further into a web of culture and history.

The Mozarabs, or 'would-be-Arabs', were Christians who retained their faith under Islamic governance in the time of Al-Andalus. In a promiscuous mingling of cultures, they became Arabised in lifestyle and language, and learnt craft and building skills from their 'conquerors'. Although the majority of the population converted to Islam, such Christians were treated with tolerance, had normal freedoms, and contributed to the Hispano-Arab civilisation that flourished for several centuries. In return for religious freedom, Christians and Jews were required to pay a special tax and there were a number of restrictions including a prohibition on the ringing of bells.

As I hesitate on the brink of the canyon, pages of the history books I've been reading seem to flutter open to lay steps beneath my feet. The artistry of the paths' engineering was inherited from the Arabs, whose systems of irrigation, astronomical observation, time measurement, and other mathematical and mechanical wonders still dazzle through the centuries. In the heyday of Al-Andalus, water was invited to flow. Books, libraries, poetry and dialogue between traditions also flourished. Ancient knowledge was revived, and streams of learning and science were liberated and synthesised by translations between Greek, Latin and Arabic. By 1031 the central authority of the Cordoban caliphate was fragmented by rival factions into 'taifa' city states, but the tradition of translation still rose with the walls of libraries in Toledo's 'School of Translators'.

Southern Spain became the European centre of material and intellectual wealth. Books whose words might contradict each other fraternised on the same shelves in the Caliphal library of Cordoba amongst the 400,000 volumes reputedly held there. (By comparison the largest library in Christian Europe at the time would have held no more than 400 manuscripts.) In her book about tolerance in Medieval Spain, *The Ornament of the World*, Maria Rosa Menocal says: 'these libraries were the monuments of a culture that treasured the Word.' She also speaks of the 'loving cultivation – some would say adoration – of language, and of poetry as the best that men did with the gift of language'.

In Al-Andalus, tolerance between religious groups was built upon the shared notion of 'dhimmi' or 'Peoples of the Book' who were to be respected, protected, cultivated. It was the book, words, and paper that allowed contradictory ideas to be read, embraced and to rub shoulders with each other. From where I stand, looking northwest across the valley and the Sierra de la Carrasca, the town of Játiva is only 40 kilometres away. In the 11th century it became the first place in Europe to manufacture paper. It was made from a paste of rice straw and flax and exported to Italy, Egypt, and the Orient, in an enormous, civilising trade. In Morocco, as a result, the paper is still named 'xativi'.

The making of a book requires investment and multiple skills – writing, translation, papermaking, printing, binding. A path must be built with an understanding of both land and human bodies. It involves surveyors and stonemasons, requires strong builders and insight into the human mind. Perhaps if we want a measure of the civility of a period or nation or community, we need to look at the importance placed on both books and the ways for pedestrians.

In October 2007, just one month before I left Scotland to start this walk, Muslim leaders had written a letter to Pope Benedict

XVI appealing for understanding and dialogue. 'If Muslims and Christians are not at peace, the world cannot be at peace. With the terrible weaponry of the modern world; with Muslims and Christians intertwined everywhere as never before, no side can unilaterally win a conflict between more than half of the world's inhabitants. Our common future is at stake. The very survival of the world itself is perhaps at stake.' They called the letter, 'A Common Word between Us and You', drawing attention to shared theological values and their expression in words from the holy books.

I enjoyed thinking that the paths that had coaxed me here, lined with pale, foot-worn stones, were redolent of a time of tolerance and pluralism – a pluralism perhaps still evident in place names and in cuisine. In late November, approaching the supposed 'season of peace', couscous was proudly declared on the menu in the Benimaurell restaurant where I warmed my hands around a cafe con leche; the village shop was raucous with Christmas lottery expectation.

This day in Valle de Laguart is part of a seven-day walk through La Marina Baja y Alta (Low and High), a mountain paradise just inland from the Costa Blanca's high rise hotels, tea dances and pavement restaurants whose photos try to describe meals without the embarrassment of words.

Beyond fifty years of package tourism, a new kind of 'conquest' has taken place in this part of Spain, an invasion of expatriates from Britain who, as Giles Tremlett calculated in his 2006 book *Ghosts of Spain*, own 450,000 properties on the Spanish costas. Close to a majority on the electoral registers of some villages, most live in their own ghettoes with 'English pubs'. They have their own daily newspaper, the 'Costa Blanca News', whose pages smell of the fear of Spanish plumbers and disgust at what they have left behind in Britain. Attracted principally by sunshine, they don't reflect the interest in cultural synthesis of the 8th century invaders.

I sat next to a table of these *conquistadores* in a village restaurant, listening to their talk of swimming pools, health issues, and builders from their own community. They struggled with the Spanish words for 'glass' and 'wine' in their exchanges with the waiter. At least, I suppose, they were eating Spanish food.

I started my walk from Relleu, a small village in the Marina Baja where I was staying at British poet Christopher North's centre, the 'Old Olive Press'. Less than 16 kilometres from the coast, it sits at an altitude of 400 metres amidst pine forest and almond and olive terraces probably first established in the time of Al-Andalus. The remains of the 11th century 'Moorish' castle sit on a hilltop which it shares with the Ermita de San Albert a little lower down. The road up to it is punctuated by the twelve stations of the cross. From a certain angle, the high silhouette of the local hill Le Figueret is embraced between two upright arms of the castle remains. Locals are convinced that Le Figueret represents a sleeping nun, her hands and feet the prominent crags along the ridge, pointing to the stars. Such are the contradictory inheritances of the place that the common greeting in the narrow streets, *Hola,* is clearly derived from 'Allah', but the village is also defined by the echo of the church bells. They ring twice on each hour for the benefit of those working out in the *campo* or countryside; the first time indicates that the hour has passed, the second time they can count the chimes.

The potency of bells as a Christian symbol was exposed in the year 997 when an evil chamberlain, al-Mansur, attacked Santiago de Compostela and removed the Cathedral bells to Cordoba to be melted down for mosque lamps. This helped elevate Santiago to mythological proportions as a Christian centre, and opened the door to hostilities. When Spanish troops went to Iraq in 2003 to join the Allied Forces, they wore the Cross of Santiago on their uniforms, otherwise know as the 'Moorslayer'.

The seven days chosen for my walk were arbitrary but gave me a satisfying measure of time. The Sunday start, when the Spanish *campo* is full of large parties of lunchers, had its own special character.

Christopher had guests for an olive-gathering weekend and I enjoyed a convivial *paella* with them in the village of Sella before setting off alone. Sunday swung around to meet Saturday, a day of hunters' gunfire in the hills, and olive gathering on the terraces. Seven days was long enough to feel the rhythm of day and night, but not so long as to be ambushed by loneliness or by lack of washing facilities in the hills.

It was an unusual season for a long walk, and confusing for a northern European. Leaves scuttled in the wind and mahogany-coloured acorns lay on the ground. There were frosts at night and only slow penetration of sun into morning valleys. But alongside these sensations came the daytime roar of bees on rosemary flowers, orange trees brilliantly laden with fruit and the air heady with the pinched sweetness of their blossom. There were grey cold days but also days of glittering blue skies. Carob pods lay in greasy heaps under trees, sunned in the afternoons into chocolate-rich scents. The light often had an Alpine brittleness that gave tangerine penumbras to the mountain silhouettes and sculpted fine wrinkles onto valley sides. This quality of light seemed to harmonise with a clarity of air that, from distant hills, ushered close the ring of voices, bells, the bark of dogs.

In the last minutes before dusk at six each evening, I would look for a camping spot on a high terrace. Overnight, my tent compressed a mattress of wild thyme into a small scented bed. The slither of plump olives down the flysheet often punctuated the hours, along with owls' calls and, frequently, the close grunts and snuffles of wild boar. When I lay down on my first night, the tent at my feet became a screen on which played the shadow puppets of pine branches tossed by wind against the full moon.

I was benighted in the tent for fourteen hours of each twenty-four. In such circumstances and alone, the choice of travel companion in book form was crucial. I couldn't have chosen better than Robert Byron's *Road to Oxiana*. He wrote about his ten-month journey to Persia and

Afghanistan in 1933 in the form of diary entries. Reportage of his conversations with officials and dignitaries often had me laughing out loud, sending the wild boar scrunching back into the forest. But he was serious too. I savoured individual sentences in which he described the unfolding of big landscapes, and colours, '...over the whole scene hangs a peculiar light, a glaze of steel and lilac, which sharpens the contours and perspectives, and makes each vagrant goat, each isolated carob tree, stand out from the white earth ....' His revelry in language converging with a search for the origins of Islamic architecture chimed with my own journey. Even though I still can't quite visualise the 'squinch' – a technique allowing a dome to be built above a square room – I love the word, and won't forget it.

Each night by head-torch, I stepped my way steadily through the pages, careful not to go too quickly and leave myself word-less. I savoured the paper – its slightly rough feel under my fingers, the wide white margin around blocks of text, the crisp flicker of a page turning. The archway of the Qur'an gate in Shiraz on its cover gave a view across domes and minarets to an impossible rise of snow-striated mountain.

This driest part of Spain became a hugely successful producer of fruit and nuts because of the ingenuity of Arab engineering that built on earlier Roman initiatives. *Secana*, or 'dry' agriculture, with its characteristic dams, channels, ponds, cisterns, waterwheels and springs, is still practised here. The construction of such systems was a technical feat but also required a massive commitment of manpower. Byron reported in Persia that, 'one third of the adult male population.... is perpetually at work on [these] underground water-channels. So developed is the sense of hydrostatics in successive generations that they can construct an incline of forty or fifty miles through almost flat country without any instruments, and at never more than a given number of feet below the ground.' Such underground systems were also installed in Madrid and Valencia, a technology that the Spanish later took to South America.

In Al-Andalus a unit of measurement was developed for irrigation based on the volume of water passing in one minute through an opening four inches high and eight wide. In the *huerta,* or irrigated area, of Orihuela, south-west of Alicante, a network of farmsteads was connected by veins of water in complex flows to and from the River Segura. Water was distributed in hourly rotations but also in a longer term rotation of 15 days.

Even today in Relleu, the system of perennial irrigation through canals and gates remains much the same. Christopher North's deeds entitle his terraces to sixteen hours' flooding a year. The distribution is managed by a local committee, and disputes are heard before the famous Court of Waters in Valencia, in existence since the year 960.

There is science in the distribution. For olive trees to flourish, the water committed within Christopher's land is exactly what is needed. The knowledge of how to manage the irrigation – by ditches hand-dug in a matrix, which are opened, flooded, and then quickly sealed off in favour of the next area – is held by the old man and his apprentice who appear on the land with spades once a year. It made me wonder how much of the technological know-how for hydropower that's buried in the mountains of my own area of Scotland, such as de-silting sluices and dams, can be attributed to Islamic engineering which worked its way north via medieval Spain.

These techniques developed early in Syria and Palestine were part of the Umayyad legacy, the 'Syrianisation' of the Spanish landscape. The effort required for terracing and irrigation was massive in relation to the scale of production, but essential to livelihoods on the land.

The terraced hillsides I walked though were a sculptural intervention as captivating as any piece of land art. Each terrace was an echo of the one before but with a subtle adjustment for the lie of the land – a tighter arc above or a longer stretch, or a spreading to accommodate a decrease in steepness. Looking at a whole hillside covered in terraces from a high point above the Valle d'Arc, I was mesmerised by how they fitted together in great arcs and cirques, one building in a spiral to the top of a conical peak. It was like watching a complex set of eddies and whirlpools in a river.

There's something of this same occult science about the paths, so strong and reliable beyond centuries of use, disuse, storm and flood. Robert Byron travelled his landscapes by a combination of horseback, car and lorry. He was rarely alone, travelling with his friend, Christopher Sykes, and sometimes with guards or servants. I walked alone, and this felt a little strange at first in an unfamiliar landscape. I wasn't always sure what to expect or whether I could trust the military maps. My doubts before setting out accumulated in direct proportion to the number of people who told me I was 'so brave'. When asked what I should be afraid of, few were specific, except for people who knew this land who mentioned wild boars, Romanian mafia, and hunters with guns.

I saw very few other walkers, but on the lower slopes I would often pass the 'hill men' pruning trees or collecting olives. In the back of their standard-issue white Citroen vans wide rubber buckets spilled olives and carob pods. The men's rust-brown overalls reminded me of the red or blue version – the uniform of men of work of the Scottish Highlands. They turned their smiles and tanned faces to me to answer questions and were generous with their knowledge of hidden paths and springs of fresh water in places where I would never have found them.

I don't know if it was Byron's influence on me, or a general intoxication because I was exerting myself and spending so much time alone, but I noticed towards the end of my journey that in my thoughts I had begun to address myself as 'we'. 'I' had become a party. On examination, I concluded that the 'we' made a distinction between my body and soul, and the things that I carried (admittedly there were quite a lot of them). My belongings were reasonably cooperative, but a rebellious pencil case containing a precious fountain pen and computer back-ups stayed behind on a mountainside on Day Three while the rest of us continued. It left me in the wilds without a writing implement.

Later that day, when I arrived in Campell, I made my usual purchases in the tiny shop – pasta, dark chocolate with almonds, manchego cheese, bread, tinned tuna. I surveyed the shelves, noting globe artichokes with plump leaves, bags of loose walnuts, tins of mussels, shoes, hand cream, condoms, and finally an ancient cardboard box which said 'BIC' on its side. Two square women who came up to my rib cage lavished smiles on me, and gave me a tangerine as a present. From the BIC box they pulled and tested black biros until one pen could be induced to run with ink. I relaxed.

They found plenty to discuss and ask about me. Was I alone? Was I camping? They noticed my walking pole which I'd telescoped down to half a metre.

'*Que es*?' one asked.

The other replied with authority: '*Es una flauta*.'

The first nodded.

I hesitated to destroy the image they'd created of me striding through the mountains playing a flute.

In Byron's jewels of landscape description, I found features of my own journey: gorges, overhanging cliffs, irrigation channels, the sudden new panorama of a distant mountain range that rewards the cresting of height. I loved the sense that we travelled through landscapes shaped by similar inheritances. His landscapes were vaster in every direction than La Marina, which covers around a thousand square kilometres of the peninsula between Valencia and Alicante, but it didn't always feel like that.

In the late afternoon on clear days, the high mountains of the Aitana range linked themselves in a blue-grey silhouette before a plummeting sun, denying separation by distance or valley, denying anything but the perpendicular. The skyline rose higher at that time of day, its profile soaring and leaping in a series of sharp pinnacles, humps and dramatic notches so that it resembled a child's cartoon version of a mountain range. I was awed by this land that I crossed.

Because my journey led me roughly north, I soon got a sense of the east-to-west orientation of the sierras. Each day I would sweat up a pass to at least 800 metres, only to descend again. Mountain, valley; mountain, valley, became my daily rhythm.

The first major pass I crossed was out of the Valle d'Arc through a narrow cleft in limestone battlements known as the Paso de los Contadores because sheep would be counted through the threshold. It led me into the Guadalest valley, luxuriant with orange trees and the fleshy leaves of the *nispero* tree. This tree bears a yellow pear-shaped fruit we know as 'loquat' that is eaten in Mediterranean countries. Introduced in the time of Al-Andalus, it's now almost a monoculture here, protected under enormous mesh screens because the fruit can be damaged by low temperatures.

Until 275,000 of them were expelled from Spain in 1609, Muslims made up the predominant community of the Guadalest valley. The village names preserve the memory – Beniarda, Benifato, Benimantell – *beni* meaning 'son of' in Arabic. At this time about one third of the population of the Valencia region were *Moriscos*, Muslims who had been forced to convert, at least nominally, to Christianity if they were to stay in Spain. Their eventual expulsion reduced the number of villages here from twenty to six, and the diversity of crops, which had included cereals, rice, and sugar cane, was gradually lost.

Tremlett's book touches on the irony of the several hundred thousand more recent Muslim immigrants to Spain, many working in these plastic-tented plantations in the south-east of the country. Their 'return' has grown a new mosque in Granada overlooking the Alhambra, but a general lack of mosques across the country, and a reluctance to allow them to be built, means that many Muslims now have to worship outside in the open air in car parks or sports fields. A Moroccan drug trade apparently helped fuel the building boom on the *Costas* and a handful of these new settlers are linked to the dark memory of the Madrid train bombings in 2004.

I often followed broad unmade roads on this journey, many in good enough condition to take a car. They sweep in great arcs to find a steady rise or fall, to avoid the deep ravines, and they make their way to the 'cracks' in the defences of long mountain ranges. Cross-country walking in this landscape is made near impossible by cataclysmic drops and by the fierce growth of gorse, kermes oaks and other spiny plants characteristic of the *garrigue* and *maquis* amongst the boulders.

After the village of Castell de Castells, heading for Laguart, my way began to incorporate short stretches of Mozarabic Trail. I knew them by character straight away. Narrow and stone-lined; polished with use but trustworthy. One side often hugs a terrace wall, while the other is marked by a low boundary of white boulders. They twist and zig-zag through steep ground, worming deep into the gloomiest parts of the gorges. They're a secret shared between those who walk and the land itself. Walkers are subsumed between terraces, disappear into the inner track of ravines and fissures. The trails are wily and direct, a welcome contrast to the broad tracks, making a virtue of the smallness and dexterity of human and animal feet. Although these short lengths didn't yet have monumental continuity, and I often found them cut across by bulldozed tracks, they always gave me a skip of delight, as if I'd made a great discovery. I found myself walking them slowly, savouring each step, admiring as I went. I added my footfall to the thorough polishing that my predecessors had given the rock.

In October this area had experienced a *Gota Fria* – a storm of wind and rain raising Monsoon proportions of water that burst cisterns, sheeted off undrained concrete and rampaged through land and streets. It gouged mud from hillsides, tumbling ancient terrace walls, levering boulders out from under soil, and spilling the result into valleys. Villages were cut off by landslips for several days. I was frequently walking through the resulting rubble. Signs of damage to the Mozarabic Trails were far fewer. Cobbles had sometimes been dislodged and juggled with, but the edging slabs nearly always remained in place.

In Valle de Laguart it's hard not to be reminded of the past and in particular Al-Azraq who ruled this area in the thirteenth century, building eighteen castles in a swathe between Alcoy in the west and Pego in the east. Famed for his blue eyes and for his bravery and diplomacy, Al-Azraq's presence is still tangible through such watchtowers in the valleys of Gallinera, Alcala, Ebo and Laguart. One of these castles used to spear up from Penon Roch, the conical summit at the eastern end of the Caballo Verde ridge now above me.

While Al Azraq went into exile in Granada in 1258, he returned for his last stand in a siege mounted against the town of Alcoy in 1276. The battle that was fought there is re-created in Alcoy each April in one of the many festivals of *Moros y Cristianos* celebrated throughout Alicante. Local people form groups of either 'Moors' or Christians and dress up exotically for mock battles amidst the fog of gunpowder and blare of band music. Whilst there is little attempt at historical accuracy, it seems that the celebrations commemorate both Al Azraq's battle in particular but also the general conquest and re-conquest played out over seven centuries. On the final day of the festival, the Christians are defeated in the morning, then following the appearance of Saint George, Al Azraq's forces are surrounded and overcome in the afternoon.

After Al-Azraq's overthrow in 1276, Jaime I apportioned land to the Christian (Mozarabic) villagers of Valle de Laguart. The *jovada* (locally know as a *juvee*) was a measure of land determined by the area that a yoke of oxen or mules could work in a day. The *juvees* given for each of the three villages were on the far side of the *barranco*. The paths that I'm now taking allowed the movement of people and goods between the farmsteads on one side and the villages, which were their economic and municipal centres, on the other. Whether they already existed as routes before this necessity is unclear, but the longevity of their use is certain. I talked to one woman whose great-grandfather, a mayor of Laguart in the early 20th century, had used the paths to walk once a week to Ebo, a town on the other side of the valley. This would have been a journey of 14 kilometres, but over 30 if he'd taken the circuitous road.

Walkers on these paths would often have been carrying heavy loads. I'm laden with a rucksack myself, and regretting it as I consider my first steep descent. Voices echo up from below me. I see three figures dazzled to black by the limestone boulders in the river bed. They're looking up towards me, admiring the shadowed route that's just carried them down. Reassured by their success, I entrust my feet to the first steps.

Soon I find an easy rhythm. Stride for stride, the steps fit me perfectly. They never force me to drop deeper or stretch further than my body's comfortable with. On each corner, steps fan out into a perfect dovetail, like pages hinging open from the spine of a book. They allow a significant drop with ease, one that my mother's knees might manage. Steps built for pathways in the Scottish Highlands are sometimes too high or widely spaced to fit a natural rhythm, and I've noticed the scuffed paths that arc around them causing erosion that the path is precisely designed to avoid. Not these.

I relax, accept the grace of the path, thanking its considerate builders with their Arabised skills, and shimmy 240 metres down towards the riverbed. What I'd been unable to see directly below me is that a switchback of the path contours across the wall from east to west (right to left as I'd stood on the brink) to link to the series of stairways. But first, it passes through a hole blown through a cliff face. It seems incredible that people had been able to plan this route in the Medieval period, working so harmoniously with the topography.

I arrive at the white boulders on the riverbed and look back up at the shadowland of cliff, crag, buttress, hidden steps, almost laughing at the ingenuity. Already the path has made the landscape seems less severe, more familiar, now that I'm cleft within it.

I could stay on the bright white floor of the dry river Ebo and follow it 'upstream', into the Barranco de Infierno where swirls of white rock rise and close in above head height like a cavern, apparently so narrow in places that a hand can be placed on each wall. I choose instead the ancient path up the other side, sculpted by people rather than water. Gasping up switchback steps on the steep sunlit wall, and then a crag-lined path through cactuses, I emerge at a restored farmstead, and, mercifully, a well.

I'm not long on this plateau of the Juvees d'Enmig before the next pair of Mozarabic Trails draw me back down into the narrow jaws of the Barranco de Infierno. Under a great cliff, the path weaves through limestone pinnacles before rising again, this time onto the Juvees Dalt. Here I choose the direct route once again that will plunge me for the final time into a finger of the ravine and back up to a point between the highest village of the three, Bennimaurell, and the pass at Gargas. I can see from where I stand that it's going to be formidably steep. Heat is simmering in the still underworld below.

The path slinks downwards through an open valley. Ruined farmsteads like broken sandy jewels are set within lush borders of miniature fern palm. Then the way becomes rockier, steepening into sets of stepped zig-zags. Amongst the foliage, sunlight greases grey boulders and highlights curious wrinkles as if the stone has been pinched by fingers into relief models of mountain ranges.

I'm down into the still white afternoon heat of the *barranco* floor. Stepped zig-zags lead me through grey-green shade up the other side, and then under a towering white cliff on the north-facing wall, behind which lurks the sun. When I reach the eastern edge of the cliff, the path screws itself into a series of tight stairways. It's like walking a series of terraces except that the turn at each end is perfectly hinged and graded for a pedestrian, almost disguising the effort of the climb. Higher, and the sun inches over the cliff's crest. It illuminates the white rocks bordering the pathway, and the luxuriant grass between the edging stones of each step. Each time I turn to walk west, the sun, diffused through tree and rock, creates a dazzling incandescence high above the steps.

At a white knobbly crag sitting proud of the wall of the ravine, 400 metres above the river-bottom, I rest to delay climbing out of this maze of ups and downs and twists and turns. The Mediterranean is in sight between interleaving spurs of the ravine. It's as if they're an incremental measure of distance, the striped detail of rock and foliage becoming less distinct, the colour more subtle. And before the drop to the Mediterranean plateau, there's the peak which Al-Azraq's castle is missing from, and with it a sense of his blue eyes watching since the 13th Century. He perhaps helped bequeath to this valley the fine engineering which has given us graceful ways to walk through a ferocious landscape.

I'd noticed a mistake when reading through the pages of the journal I was keeping. I'd written that I would be 'walking' a particular book. Of course I had intended to write 'reading'. When I came across this error I didn't correct it, I rather liked the analogy – the pages of a walk, the steps of a book. It seems appropriate to this particular walk that still rustles with people who placed value on dialogue and tolerance and embodied it in books and words.

Books were seen as a threat to the single-nation, single-religion state that was subsequently established here. After 1492, when Jews were expelled from Spain if they refused to be baptised, and the last Muslim stronghold of Granada was taken by Isabella and Ferdinand, the burning of libraries speaks for the power of paper, pages and words. The new rulers wanted rid of contradictions inscribed in literatures. It seems an act of vandalism and division that we're still suffering from, reflected in the minimal dialogue between literatures of West and East.

Arab culture led translation in the 8th and 9th centuries, making ancient Greek and Latin texts accessible and helping bring about Europe's renaissance. Yet the UN estimates that the entire number of books translated into Arabic in the past 1,000 years is the same as that translated into Spanish in a single year. Literary translation from Arabic into English has grown in the last decade, averaging 10-

16 works a year. However it remains largely the preserve of specialist publishers, driven by interest in socio-political commentary rather than a desire to explore the literary culture of the Middle East and North Africa. It seems folly not to cultivate understanding at a time of much-needed dialogue.

Maria Rosa Menocal, in summarising the long-term influence of Al-Andalus writes of, 'the hope that stories can bring, since by their very nature they resist clear-cut interpretations and are likely to reveal the different ways in which truths and realities can be perceived. In its insistence that the point of stories, of literature, is to pose difficult questions rather than to propose easy answers or facile morals, this tradition is a central part of the Andalusian legacy to subsequent European culture.'

Two nights after I leave Valle de Laguart, having doubled back towards the south-eastern part of La Marina, (collecting the deviant pencil case on the way) I camp in the shadow of a high promontory which guards a steep twist of ravine before dropping to the River Bolulla. I'm overlooked by a castle that tops the promontory. It's another of Al-Azraq's; square, sand-coloured and enduring. The muscle of the mountain, its bulk and invincibility seems to have been thrust into that castle-top.

When I wake the next morning, the grunts and scuffles of my night visitors are long gone. But a slick of moon hangs bright behind me in the west and a star still pricks the sky above the castle. I wait for the traces of night to fade. I look again for the spring marked on my map that I searched for in half-light last night. I used my remaining water to cook up pasta and went to sleep dehydrated, with my face roaring from too much sun. But I fail again to find the spring. This is my last day of walking and I begin to feel the need to eat properly, to spread out a bit, perhaps even to speak to some people and get clean. My socks smell like an intensive chicken farming unit. But the trajectory towards comfort is still hanging in a balance with the desire to continue the journey.

Robert Byron knew this feeling. Remembering that his journey is nearly over as he approaches Kabul, he reflects: 'The getting up at four, cooking porridge over a wood fire, ordering food for our meagre picnic outfit in its battered Persian tin, seeing the lamps are filled in case of a night in the open, jumping out to fill the water-bottles at every spring, cleaning our boots every other day, and rationing the men with cigarettes to keep them happy, have become an automatic routine; and the thought that tomorrow it will cease leaves us flat and a little melancholy.'

As it will be hours before the sun penetrates my wrinkle in the hill, I pack up the wet tent, crystals of frost melting against my hands. I take my time, enjoying the ricochet of a band of crows from one side of the ravine to the other, their high cries echoing and following them from wall to wall. Soon afterwards, the cries are replaced with the sharp, repeated ring of gunshots. It's Saturday.

My numb fingers rush back to life as I burst into sunlight on the crest of the Paso Tancat. Suddenly a new, but familiar, view spreads itself below me – the cling-film wrapped glitter of the Guadalest valley where *nisperos* are grown, and the end of my walk. I pause before the long descent. After taking advice from a hill-man tinkering in a collapsing farmstead, I resolve to 'storm' the castle from the pass.

Pushing to the back of my mind my dehydrated state, and abandoning my rucksack, I scramble up its eastern slopes. There are remnants of a circular tower constructed from pale gold stone cemented in rough rows with a few sight-holes. A long narrow summit with a precipice on each side leads me to the remains of a rectangular chamber. The walls have fallen in and been covered by grass so that it seems less substantial, its sides lower than they looked from a distance. Its height and inaccessibility made it forbidding, but the all-but-invisible seam between man-made fortress and natural rock would have assisted this impression.

Beyond the castle is a further, lower, promontory that rises directly above the fiercesome twist and drop into the *barranco*. But there's only a knife edge between it and the castle. Even so I hear bells tinkle and see the outlines of white goats. They look two-dimensional, two-legged, and as still as the precipice which seems to hold them at odd angles. Byron's account of climbing to the Sassanian castle Kali-i-Dukhtar near Ibrahimabad, comes to mind: 'Seen from behind, the castle stands on a promontory and is thus defended on three sides by precipices that fall almost sheer from its outer walls.' I feel rewarded, sharing something that's been created here with links across time and geography and still standing defiant after nine centuries.

I look to the south, where today's way becomes more road-like, taking slow arcs down and down until the promontory will tower 900 metres over me, and I'll then follow the river to the village of Bolulla.

I can see back to my near-starting point at Paso de los Contadores on the far side of the Guadalest valley where Muslim settlers created luxuriant life and growth with patterned terraces and measured water. They're there now, tending the loquats, and probably living without a dedicated place to worship. As I sit on Al-Azraq's hill-top, the sound of another type of bell rises. Not goat bells. The church tower chiming midday in Bolulla.

The bells summon me. The gunshots drive me away. I'm cowering from the naked sun, the back of my mouth sticky and slow, and the skin of my face sultana-dry. I head down; down into the tinkling valleys with questions still ringing in my mind.

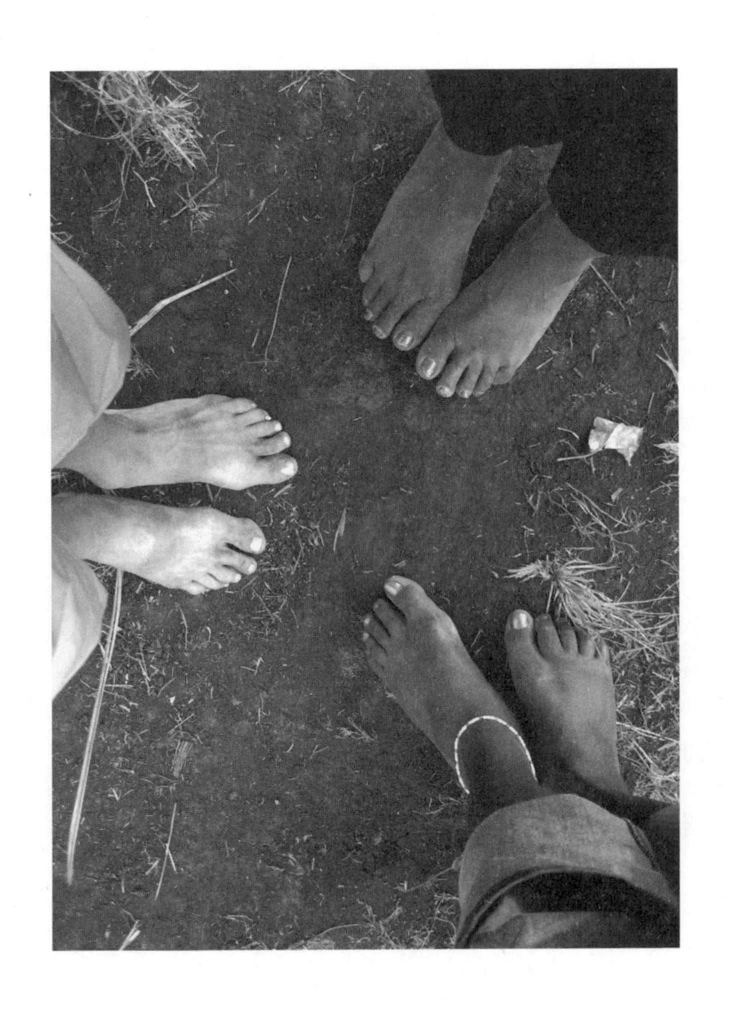

Baring our Soles

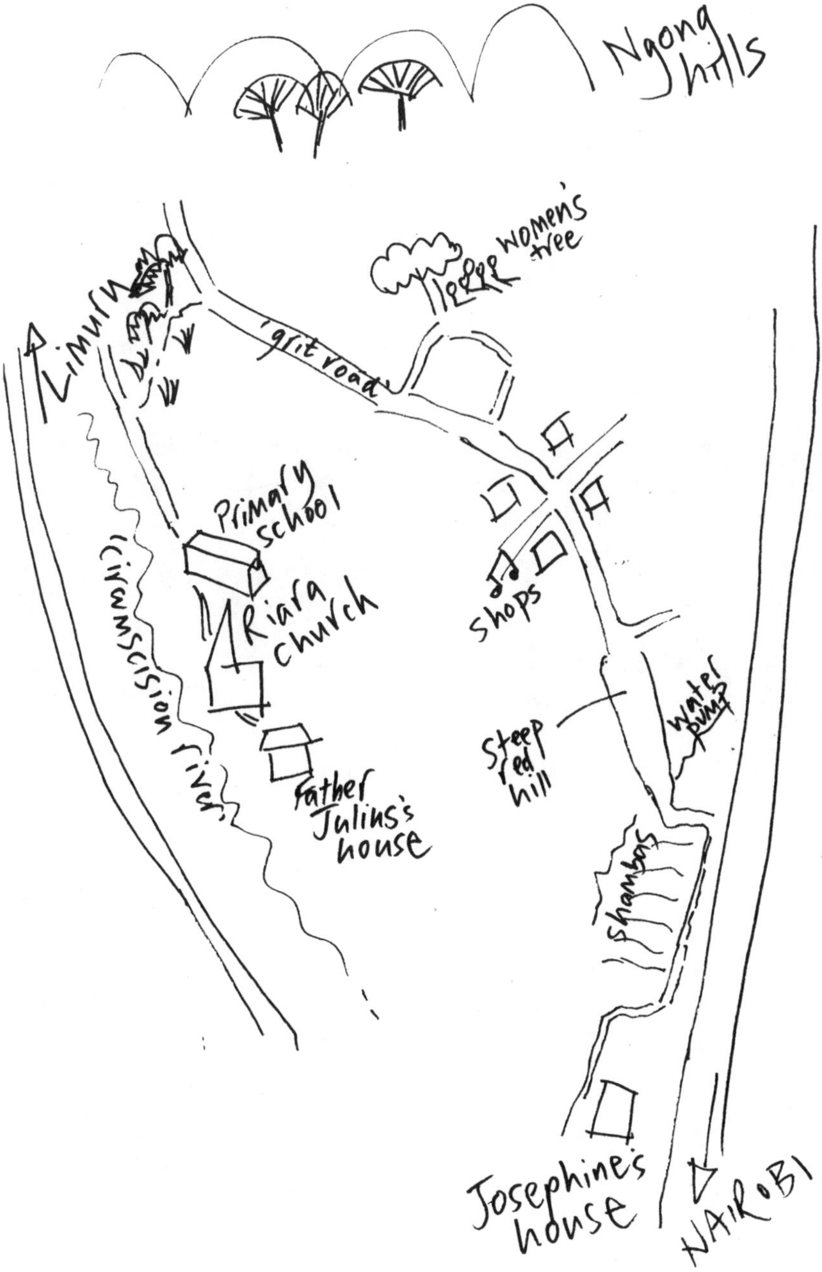

Ngong hills
women's tree
Limuru
'grit road'
Primary school
Riara church
Shops
Circumscision river
Father Julius's house
Steep red hill
water pump
shambas
Josephine's house
NAIROBI

Ndumberi Village
Kiambu County
Central Kenya

The path is made by walking
African Proverb

'Are you on strike?' a man called after us. He gave us an excuse to pause while we laughed and shook our heads.

Philo, her young friend Renée, and I had arrived in Philo's village by car, wearing sunglasses and clutching at mobile phones that linked us to faster worlds in Nairobi and beyond. Now our shoes were off and we were walking gingerly, exposing ourselves to good-humoured curiosity.

Walking barefoot can have multiple meanings – from penance to pilgrimage to protest and empowerment to poverty and powerlessness. But it also has a sensory impact.

'When you have your shoes on you're one station removed from being yourself,' Philo had said that morning, while we talked about our walking experiences and she recalled her barefoot village walks as a girl. She compared it to separation from the land when we travel by car. 'When you walk barefoot it's like you're talking. There's something that goes on between your body and the earth.'

I first met Philo Ikonya in Senegal in 2007 at a conference of the international organisation, PEN, which unites writers in a concern with freedom of expression. We coincided while out for morning walks and discovered common ground as we talked of writing and human rights and our lives. Her fierce intelligence and humour danced through memorable talk that made sisters of us despite the difference in our backgrounds. It was while still in Senegal that we planned to walk together around the village where Philo grew up, but we'd decided only today to go barefoot, for simple pleasure and to see what meaning we could draw from the sensations.

The man's question about us striking was not surprising. The bare feet of city visitors to these lush-leafed, peopled ridges just to the north of Nairobi might well speak a political language in January 2009. Exactly a year before, disastrous elections had resulted in violence that left over a thousand people dead, thousands injured and some 300,000 displaced. The growing of maize was disrupted leading to a famine, and now a major scandal was erupting as maize imported to alleviate the situation had reportedly been sold to South Sudan. A shaky coalition government was setting the streets murmuring with discontent, and all secondary school teachers were on strike – we'd seen them marching barefoot in several places on our travels, waving branches above their heads.

It was a long time since I'd walked barefoot anywhere except on a beach, but I was willing to try. Philo had told me that women and girls all go barefoot on these village paths. The rainy season transforms the hard red earth into a clogging swamp and shoes are completely impractical. But for me and for my friends used to wearing shoes in Nairobi's streets, it was strange and difficult.

We weren't going far, simply teasing out some paths around the village to celebrate a web of journeys made over fifty years by Philo, her siblings and particularly her mother, and to chart changes with our feet. Of these intersecting paths and roads and the domestic landmarks that linked them, Philo had said before we came here, 'all that area is deeply related to my family'. From her mother's house we would walk to the river where water was collected, to the school where her mother taught for thirty years, and finally to Riara church which was so emblematic of their family life because all ten children had been baptised there.

When we met Philo's mother, Josephine Wambui Ikonya, her feet had looked strong, lying parallel beneath her on the tiled floor of her house. They were shapely, with a slightly blueish-grey hue, the left one still bruised and swollen where a rock had fallen on it the week before. Nevertheless they suggested confidence in themselves.

Josephine's composed figure on the sofa with its purple and orange crocheted cover, had gathered the room in around her, drew our eyes and attention to her. The hands crossed on her lap were wide and workish on the slim wrists of a woman so small that when she stood up she barely reached my chest. They were hands that still cut maize and dug soil on the *shamba*, the plot where food is grown. She wore a blue and white silk scarf over her hair. Her face was enlivened by dark eyes, a small sharp nose, and full lips which when broadening into a smile showed a gap between her front teeth and carved her face into angularity; a miniature version of Philo's beauty.

A gallery of popes and madonnas hung from a high rail and were spread on an altar-like table along with photos of the family. As we walked out into the lush garden of broad banana leaves, Philo pointed out the graves of a number of family members including several children. Keingati had died aged two in the 1950s and his beauty rang through the family's memory and still seemed to define them; he was often referred to as the angel of the family. As tradition determined, he was 're-born' when a later son was given his name.

We'd already seen a photo of Philo's brother Peter, at his graduation from Northern Alberta Institute of Science and Technology, who had died aged only thirty-five. She told me a little of him and how the two often walked these village paths together. Affection and loss animated her description of his distinctive footprint. It was inherited through her mother's family who she said walked with 'amazing feet'. Philo described the shape of the heel as a zero, with an arch so high that the foot didn't meet the ground again until the next little zero at the ball and the 'dot, dot, dot' of the toes. She would know his footprint anywhere, she said, printed onto the earth paths radiating from the house, layered now under the marks of more recent walkers.

On the lane leading away from Josephine's house, the three of us stood in a circle and looked at our feet. Renée's dark smooth skin contrasted with pale pink nail polish and a white-beaded anklet; Philo's were lighter brown with a slight map of veins and dark pink nails; my nails were painted silver, the skin of my feet already dusted darker with red soil. Renée and Philo's feet looked broad and strong, so much more reliable than my thin, bony, pale pair. We turned our feet over to compare the soles and found they were all the same colour.

At first our feet reflexed away from the ground in fear of sharp pebbles that cars had scrambled up. Neighbours hailed our small sisterly procession as we crept onwards. Philo was well known to the village people. She not only grew up here but stood for parliament in this constituency the previous year. I'd taken a photo of her in Senegal. She was half-turned towards me with a wide open-lipped smile and her hair was swept up into a colourful cloth band that matched her dress in a bold print of blue, yellow, and green. The photo had been chosen to illuminate her election campaign – a face so full of life on flyers and roadside posters that it made people ask: 'Is this election a beauty pageant?'

She was famous for her grass-roots activism, for hard-hitting journalism attacking corruption and injustice, and for campaigns addressing basic needs, especially for women. During the worst days of unrest in 2008, she'd walked the streets of Nairobi wearing a sackcloth to draw attention to the plight of her beloved country.

The people of Kiambu knew Philo had promised miracles if she was elected: an education that would allow them to stand on their own two feet and thereby ensure access to shelter, food, clothing and medicine.

'But,' they said as they smiled us past. 'Look at her powers now. She can even make a white woman walk without shoes!'

We tackled the steep, stony path down to the river cautiously, until we reached some large water-worn rocks over which our soles curled and lingered for their smoothness and warmth. Philo told us how the river used to reach up to the rocks. She recalled the excitement of crossing it on stepping stones, how its rapid flow made it seem a great fountain, alive with beetles, she said, frog spawn, even once a large green snake that dashed across the surface. She finds it diminished now by global warming, by planting of the wrong trees, by damming upstream and the discharge of chemical waste.

A small stretch of our legs, and we'd stepped over it, saw it trickle greyly away downstream through heart-shaped leaves of taro root.

A little upstream was the pipe where the girls of Philo's family came to collect water, and where a small gang were now doing the same. Philo stopped to talk, always a story-gatherer, always wanting to know about the lives of ordinary people who she met as she walked.

In the late 80's, I spent a year living and working in Zanzibar – an island off the coast of Tanzania a few hundred kilometres south east of Nairobi - and I explored by bicycle and when possible, on foot. My affection grew for the way of life there, including the routine of walking which I found made an easy way of meeting people as well as giving me a better sense of geography. Following foot-beaten earth paths, or polished coral rag, I pieced together cross-country walks from one village to another. From one bay where mangrove poles had been cut and lashed into bundles ready for collection, into another where fishermen prepared their boats, these were busy, peopled ways, alive with industry and the carriage of tools or fish or vegetable produce. I loved the sense that even in rural places, people walked in order to get somewhere.

Being a pedestrian was a social activity there, rarely a solitary one, and I was never allowed to lose my way. One set of directions – part told and gestured by waves of the hand, or very often accompanied –

linked to the next. The word *mzungu* for a white person, comes from a Swahili verb *kuzunguzungu* which means to feel dizzy, an observation of the habit of white people to walk in circles. Usually the people I met laughed when I asked for directions, said it was too far for an *mzungu* and pointed me towards the road where Europeans belonged, where cars changed the scale of the land and left roadside walkers and traders blinded by dust.

Philo took a full canister of water from a small girl and carried it, panting under its weight, up the steep red hill ahead. It lay across her back and shoulders as she braced and pushed against the harness of a twine head-strap. The girl walked by her side, her body leant away from the weight of a similar-sized barrel that she carried in one hand, her face and neck taut with the strain. When the path levelled out and met a dirt road curling in from the right, the barrels were lowered to the ground to await collection by a hand-drawn cart.

'This is the shopping centre', Philo said as we reached a small shack from which loud music and portions of chips were issued to a gathering of adults and children. The children tried out on me their chorus of 'how are you?'. Some quietly told me their names. One boy smiled and propelled forward the wire-framed vehicle he'd built as a toy. It was an articulated lorry, its eight wheels made from medicine pots. It was to be admired, and we did so.

Just near the corrugated iron kiosks selling bundles of charcoal and onions, an old woman in a bright orange pleated skirt stopped to talk to us. I didn't understand the words between her and Philo in Kikuyu and passed the minutes hopping from one foot to the other as my soles were scorched by the baked soil of the afternoon road.

'She says she walks from Nairobi to here barefoot,' Philo said, of the thirty or so kilometres we had just driven. The woman's feet were dark grey in colour with thickened heels. She was standing still, not seeming to feel the heat.

'She says she can perfectly well afford to buy shoes, but why would she not want to walk barefoot?' Philo signalled the smooth red earth, the maize and coffee plants lifting in the breeze, the absence of vehicles.

I wondered how the woman's walk would be interpreted in Nairobi, where, as Philo had said earlier, 'the city ways are hostile to barefoot travellers'. Would people read poverty rather than pleasure in her steps?

The woman gave us a final greeting and then walked away at an even, stately pace. My progress behind her was slow, my head bent as I concentrated on the next footfall.

As we approached a junction, I could hear a growing hubbub, a constant murmuring like a stream falling over rocks. The source eventually came into view. About thirty women were seated straight-legged and close together on a grass verge, heads covered in colourful scarves. We greeted them and they answered noisily, talking to Philo in Kikuyu, which she later translated for me. One of the women was a lifelong friend of Philo's mother, and explained that this was their weekly meeting. The women told Philo they had problems using the ground they were sitting on because a spurious ownership was being claimed. As far as they were concerned, it was public land. They were resisting intimidation.

They fell into silence as Philo addressed them. In each pause in her encouragement to them, they answered her emphatically and in one voice, a gust of breath, a nasal 'hey', which seemed to indicate agreement and understanding.

Then Philo asked me to talk to them in my stuttering Swahili, and I told them I'd come from Scotland to walk here. I waggled a foot in illustration, at which they laughed. It was often in meetings such as these, in chance discussions with groups of people on food stalls or in the *bunge* street parliaments, that I saw Philo's skill in nurturing people's desire for change.

We crossed onto a wide road, the 'grit road' as Philo called it, walking next to a maize field and then coffee blossoming white to our left. The road was busy with a tide of people carrying their loads from the fields. I was mostly watching my feet. They sought the highest, most polished humps from which pebbles had been swept, and my toes stretched upwards, seeking air, moving in a way they don't in shoes. It was as if they'd developed a new articulacy, and had come alive.

Children followed us, giggling and chatting quietly between themselves.

Philo laughed. 'When they write their novels, they'll have a white woman walking barefoot, the image is so strong for them.'

She was leading us across a high plateau now. Ahead of us a drop in the road revealed an expanse of forest rising to the misty heights of the Ngong Hills. An acacia tree was silhouetted on the horizon, its distinctive curved canopy like a portion of cartwheel. Just on the skyline of the dropping road, a horizontal mass of leaf and stem ten feet wide appeared, shuddering slowly uphill. At each end the maize nearly touched the ground. Another bundle followed it. Gradually, as the apparitions rose towards us, slight legs were revealed below the centre of each load and eventually we saw that two women were bent beneath them, heads obscured. It looked like a kind of punishment, but when we drew level with them, their greetings, through audible panting, were cheerful enough. Then they turned up an alley and disappeared into a compound, the hairy maize heads catching and shivering against fences as they went.

A few raised islands of ageing tarmac met our feet. Its frogspawn lumpiness touched a memory on my sole of a time when I'd found it liberating to walk barefoot. It was a summer in the mid 1970s when I was in the sixth form and released from school uniform. Influenced by hippy culture and a long hot summer, I wore floor-length flowery skirts. Hidden beneath them as I walked the mile to and from school, my feet were bare, the soles hardening day by day against warm tarmac. If I could get away with it I stayed barefoot throughout the day, pacing the cool tiles of the school corridors between classes, a pair of rubber flip-flops carried in my bag in case I was challenged. I loved my tough feet then.

I thought of Alexandra Stewart's account of living in Glen Lyon in Perthshire in the early twentieth century. She recalls a social, sensual way of walking, even in a cold climate: 'Although my father was a shoemaker we went to school barefoot from late spring to early autumn. The road was good to walk on. It was not tarmac but a soft, dusty surface, easy for horse traffic and kind to the feet. Many a time we were sent to school with boots on and hid them in a convenient hole in the wall, to be collected on our way home. It was three miles to the school. We always met other children on our way and groups of us trooped together. Most of us went barefoot.'

I'm inclined to ignore my feet, especially in the winter. They'd been bundled up in recent weeks, even as I sat at my desk, or crammed into boots when I'd gone out, boots that seemed to make unbending planks of them, as if appending their natural function with something more useful. I'd looked at them with distaste in the bath – the thickening yellow toenails suggesting fungal infection, the puffy arthritic joint of the left big toe. And now they'd been released to this!

Abandoning the road for a narrow path to our left, we dropped steeply into a valley through a high corridor of foliage. Our feet padded silently on the soil still damp and cool with the memory of last week's rain. The path opened out to reveal a mosaic of small plots, whose colours and textures were determined by their crops: maize, banana and the wide blades of fast-growing Napier grass for cattle. A ridge rose beyond the valley and a spire peeked through a gap between trees.

Up on the ridge, a gateway opened into the primary school where Philo's mother had worked. I picked my way through dumped rubble. Philo looked around at the single storey brick-built classrooms, grills at the windows clinging onto shards of broken glass, the doors swinging open. She wanted to know what had happened since she'd last come, why one of the classrooms was condemned, what should be done? I sensed one of her campaigns developing.

Looking into the valley beyond the ridge, she pointed to what she called the 'circumcision river'. When she was young, pubescent girls were brought here to sit in the water, anaesthetising their genitals prior to cutting, a custom that was rejected by her own parents. It's a rite of passage far less commonly marked by knives now, more often with words. Two women were washing clothes there, the flow of a remembered river barely visible amidst green meadows.

We moved through another gate and met the plain face of Riara Church. Solid, tall and white, the alcoves of its circular and arched windows were edged in pale turquoise. Despite the complaints of our feet, a celebration was suggested as the sun sank lower, flushing up deep colours and casting long shadows from an umbrella tree. A journey was complete; a ritual fulfilled.

A novice invited us into the garden of Father Julius' house where we rested in a gazebo amidst ornamental shrubs and the scent of rosemary. The young man wore a sweatshirt from the Oldmachar Academy in Aberdeen with its motif of three fishes and a tower – one of those strange folds in geography that carry a hint of home. Philo then recalled a blind Scotsman, Father Wallace, who used to walk from here. If challenged on it, he would always refute that he was alone, saying he was walking with his 'great friend, The Holy Ghost'.

In turn the three of us washed our feet under the garden tap. The red soil streamed away, the water cooled hot soles, gilded our feet with sunlight. We put on our shoes again. My soles tingled, and as we started back, my gait was shifted by the elevation from the ground. A new perspective, a sense perhaps closed off, but I felt deeply refreshed.

It had taken us two and a half hours to get to the church, slowed by our soft soles, detours and conversations, pauses for reflection. Our return took little more than thirty minutes, the valley half kissed by golden light and half leaned over by shadows, its sides cupping the cries and small startled journeys of weaver birds.

We found Philo's mother sitting on her sofa, hands folded, strong feet still firmly planted. As darkness shrank the neighbourhood around the house, we drank tea, ate bread spread with Blue-Band, chewed newly-harvested sweet maize from its cob.

I showed Josephine the photographs I'd taken.

'What memories we'd be able to have with photos such as these,' she said.

We looked at her wedding photo. She was twenty, seated in a white satin dress with tiny capped sleeves. On her lap those calm hands held flowers. Her face, the dark points of her deep-set eyes, were completely recognisable sixty years on. Her husband stood next to her in a white suit, as handsome as she was beautiful, a slight nervousness betrayed by the uneven weight on his feet.

I wondered about her feet, whether in the contours and cracks of the skin, her soles would reveal a map in miniature of the ways we'd just taken, the well-worn routes between home and river; home and workplace; home and church?

Philo was excited when we met the next day. Having seen how our walk attracted attention, and how we'd felt so energised by it, she'd made some phone calls. A group of writers and activists would walk barefoot through Nairobi. Their feet would write a protest at this important time in Kenya's history.

In mid February before their walk happened, I returned to a Scotland locked into a ferocious cold snap. Footprints radiated out from the town where I live, etching into deep snow an archive of journeys made by dog-walkers over several days. Even after an aggressive thaw, the raised islands of impacted boot-prints remained, stamped in lines across the grass like floating reminders of journeys made in a different climatic age. I thought of the red dust paths of Philo's village, worn by successive generations.

My eyes caught on a full-page advert in a magazine. The text read: 'Shoes are eroding the backbone of our society. Disguised as harmless footwear, these traitors have colluded with hard, flat surfaces to strike a crippling blow to our posture. But there is a form of resistance that will save our spines from utter destruction.' Astonished at this apparent promotion of barefoot walking, I was then puzzled to see an image of a fat-soled shoe and the letters 'MBT' at the bottom of the page – 'Maasai Barefoot Technology'. I thought of various Maasai people I'd recently met, who were either barefoot or in flip-flops, and wondered what they would make of it.

As I walked and read and settled back to a comfortable winter melancholy, I thought back over my experiences in Kenya. They included the desire for peace, political freedom and tolerance I'd seen in people everywhere I went with Philo; and a hunger for books and reading which by and large remained un-met. We'd visited Kisumu in the west of Kenya, and celebrated in 'Obama's' village, Kogelo, on the day of his Presidential inauguration. We'd hoped to sell the book that Philo had written for young readers about Obama's Kenyan origins. We spent the day surrounded by children, and often adults, devouring the pages of the book. But it was unthinkable for any of these 'country folk' to buy a copy, or even get access to one to borrow, a situation reflected all over sub-Saharan Africa where any available books, even in school libraries, are so precious they might be wrapped in plastic and kept on a shelf rather than read.

I thought about libraries and their power, so tangibly evident in the impulse of Spanish rulers to destroy them at the end of Al-Andalus. And I remembered Innerpeffray, Scotland's first public lending library that had enchanted me for so long, set on a bend of the river Earn in Perthshire. Founded in 1680 after a long period of terrible violence in Scotland, it epitomises Scotland's Enlightenment and a belief in the power of books to civilise and democratise, to illuminate the spirit. Its use by local people – stonemasons, maids, dyers – who walked miles to reach the library, reflected a passion for learning. More recently a magnet for literary tourists rather than a lending library, I'd wanted to write something set there for a long time.

Parallels began to form in my mind. Along with them came the character of an enthusiastic Kenyan librarian from the Kisumu area, personally affected by the post-election violence, who is exploring British libraries on a study visit and becomes enchanted himself by Innerpeffray. An idea for a radio play began to emerge out of two very different landscapes and sent me scurrying for pen and paper.

Then an urgent email arrived from a member of PEN Kenya. Philo had been arrested during a peaceful protest outside Parliament. Her hands had been raised in empty maize packets to highlight the hunger of ordinary Kenyans brought about through corruption.

News trickled in over the hours:

She was in a police cell.

She was in court.

She was in hospital following her brutal treatment by the police.

Then she was home and safe.

Immediately after release and before sleep, she posted her experience on her blog, including the stories of women she met in the cells who had less leverage to be fairly treated; raising her voice for the voiceless.

One detail particularly saddened me. As she was moved by the police from station to cell to court, provoked with punches, verbal abuse, threats; as she was walked between cars, cells and interview rooms, with keys shaken, heavy bolts drawn on dark rooms with light bulbs that didn't work; the police had taken away her shoes. She was barefoot.

My own feet still recalled our walk; some of the toughened skin was peeling off in a translucent film grained with contours. I enjoyed the sensation, the visceral reminder of the meeting of our skin with the skin of the earth. But it took on a different meaning now.

'It's one thing to love to walk village paths barefoot,' Philo wrote in an email afterwards, 'another to be forced to step on cold cement... Our feet celebrations turned into tears'. She compared it to the humiliation of being stripped.

There were verbal threats too, insinuations; the most vicious part of the treatment. When one of the policemen said: 'Madam, do you know how you will die?' she answered: 'Yes; surrounded by books, in my bed, with people that love me.'

The police released her with only one shoe. The day after leaving hospital she walked back across the City, barefoot and defiant, carrying the one remaining shoe to demand its pair at the police station.

Showing shock in their faces, people stopped to ask her if she was protesting about something.

'Yes,' she said. This time, she was.

Following our fathers

Château de Lavigny, Switzerland, August 2012

In the early days here when I looked beyond Lac Léman towards the Alps, they were lost in cloud and haze; remote and sketchy. When the cloud cleared slightly and low sunlight highlighted crags and revealed a saddle covered in snow, I was almost tempted to consult a map and give names to the peaks. But I turned my back. The daily sound of cow bells in the fields below the Château tease up memories of Alpine walking and ring with the painful lure of the hills. But I still hope to resist. Being here to sit down and write, I've deliberately come unequipped for a mountain expedition.

This morning I walked to the north of Lavigny, plunging into a little tree-filled valley where a stream gurgles past Moulin Martinet, and then, when I followed it downstream, Moulin au Loup. After a night of rain, the cloud was breaking and the sky was mottled soft grey and blue. I climbed up a small hill south of Villars to reach the path that would return me to Lavigny, dodging stretched-out slugs intent on crossing the track. Just at the hill's crest, with ranks of maize to my right and woodland to my left, I came to a standstill. A great wall of powder-blue sky ahead of me shifted, rearranged itself, and with a lurch of something like longing, I realised that I wasn't looking at sky but at the silhouettes of mountains, high and serrated. It was as if, having remained quiet and unnoticed for long enough, they'd stood up to their full height and asked, 'Well? What about it, then?'

I began my love affair with mountains when I was seven and my mother 'accidentally' took myself, and my older brother and sister up Snowdon. She'd only intended us to walk a short distance up the path, but my brother started to cry every time she tried to turn us around. It was memorable for the blizzards that flushed my nose into a continuous stream, and a trail of Rolos left on cairns that lured us to the summit railway station. The idea was to descend by train, but we found it wasn't running because of snowdrifts. That first mountain experience gave me the determination needed later for Snowdonian peaks on school 'Adventure Weeks'.

My twenties and thirties were punctuated by Scottish summits in every kind of weather condition, and some fairly cowardly rock-climbing. I was always slightly afraid of the high, sometimes hostile places reached, but thrilled too by the elemental force of it, the views, and by a sense of achievement. For me, such trips were about climbing out of the trivia and pressure of everyday life, escaping the largely human world for a shift of scale.

These next two stories tell of walks amongst mountains in Norway and Switzerland but they are also journeys of discovery; a search for two fathers lost to their daughters as children. It was the first, following the route of a friend's father's life or death wartime journey, that set me off to 'double back' on many of the paths in this book. It showed me how profound it felt to use my body to re-tell someone's story. After that I became less intent on walking to 'get away from it all' and more interested in walking those paths that beat with a human resonance. The Norwegian walk also made me realise the need for a second journey connecting walking and memory. I strongly suspected that I'd inherited from my father my inability to spend a whole day indoors, especially if the sun was shining.

So I found that the time had come to discover *his* mountains.

Pappa's Shoes

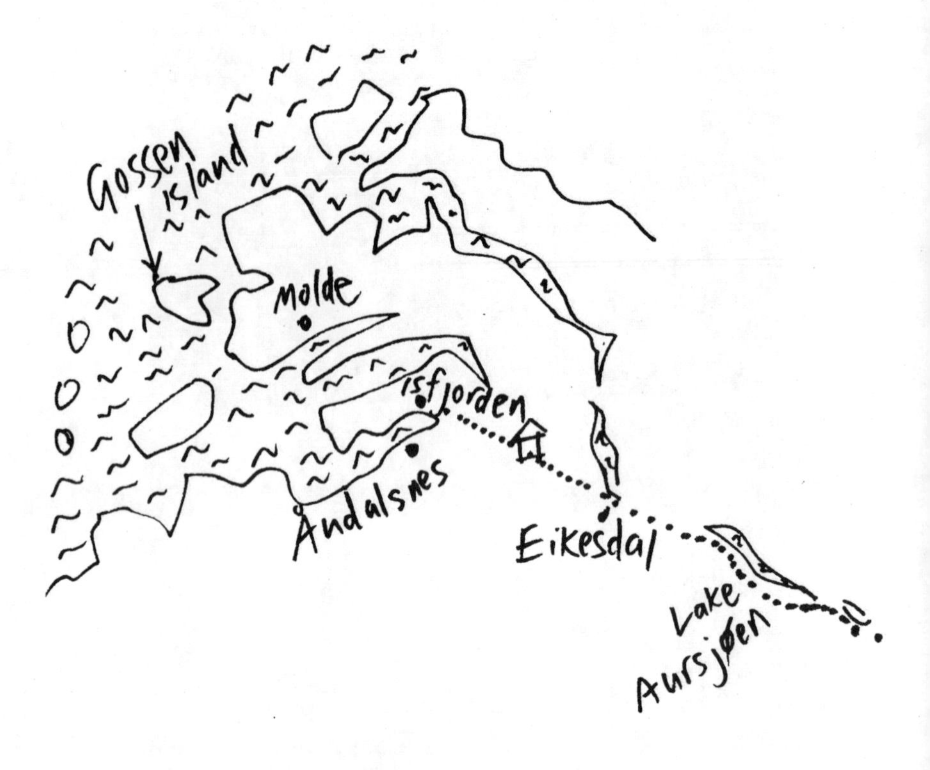
Gossen Island
Molde
Isfjorden
Åndalsnes
Eikesdal
Lake Aursjøen

NORTH

DOVREFJELL

Fokstugu

Dombås

RONDANE HILLS

Swedish border

Engerdal

Lake Atnsjøen

Lillehammer Gjøvik

A wartime escape route

Norway

People should be encouraged to walk in the hills. It will increase their attachment to their country.

Raja Shehadeh, *Palestinian Walks*

I take off my new walking boots and leave them with others at the door of Selma Moldsvor's house at Isfjorden. The village sits at the far end of one of the fingers of sea that penetrate deep inland between Alesund and Molde. From the window of the sun-washed living room, the Romsdal Alps are sparring high into a July sky, the light dancing off rock and the determined, late-lying patches of snow. The hills tremble with promise.

Our group of five is absorbed into a gathering of crag-faced elderly men – once climbers – and journalists. Ellie, the eldest of the Sømme siblings, chats with them in Norwegian about what I assume to be plans for our walk. My old friend Yuli, and her brother Bertie hover on the edges of this, their grasp of the language slighter because they were very young when the family left Norway in 1962. Ellie's twenty-three year-old son Oliver and I are like children, not comprehending what will happen next.

The five of us are expecting to start walking from Selma's house, but the hours talking rather than walking are creeping us into the afternoon. The focus of our trip so far has been on meeting people rather than the practical details of the journey. I have little idea of the daily distances planned, or the amount of food we need to carry before reaching the next shop. I try to bury my frustration, wait for the moment when I can breathe the mountain air and get my arms and legs swinging. I want to put my boots back on.

I met Yuli in 1982, at a spinning and weaving gathering in Devon where we both then lived. She was wearing one of those traditional Norwegian cardigans – snowflake patterned, fastened with pewter clasps. I was drawn to her calmness and slightly foreign beauty, and her passion for working with wool – something that I was learning about at the time. We became friends, later sharing a house and working in the same woollen museum. Then I moved to Scotland in 1990 and we saw each other rarely.

I had always known about her Norwegian father, who, like mine, died when she was very young. I'd seen the Norwegian flag displayed on the wall of her mother's house. The hand-written caption beneath it read: 'Flag carried by Sven Sømme when he escaped from the Germans in June 1944'.

Sixty years later, his family decided to set off in his footsteps. Well in advance Yuli invited me to accompany them – we'd finally be able to spend time together and I could contribute my experience of long-distance walking. She sent me a series of seven photocopied maps and Sven's own account of his journey, which was produced in the 1970s as a small book, *Biologist on the Run* (Re-issued in 2005 as *Another Man's Shoes*). She'd translated his route from words into a line of green ink that traversed each map. In places, the line was broken, and question marks interrupted the certainty. On the back of Map One she had written a note to say that one section of the map was missing, and she wrote an encouragement: 'I can't help saying it but I do hope you can come'.

For a reason I couldn't put my finger on, I remained uncommitted to joining the party as the Sømmes made their plans and got themselves fit. Perhaps it was just my own lack of connection to the story. Despite the lines and contours and place names in black and white, the landscape remained entirely mysterious and intangible to me. It was the first expedition I'd considered since separating from Neil, my partner since our early 20s, with whom I'd been on many of my mountain walks. I didn't feel confident. I was lured by the idea of being outdoors, the mountains, the new experience that Norway would give me, but tugged back by a need for home, comfort, the steady revolution of familiar, easy paths.

In the end, about ten days before departure, I gave in to the former impulse, and decided to go with them.

The first few days in Norway unmoored me from my everyday world, while I waited for our walk to start. We travelled through landscapes half-Scottish and familiar, half strange, growing more spectacular as the train climbed from Oslo north-west through castellated pinnacles where trolls are said to lurk, down to the towns which crouch on convoluted coastlines amidst a complex jigsaw of sea, island and mountain.

As a broadcaster herself, Ellie's advance publicity had been highly effective in alerting the Norwegian media and brought forward many people who had been involved in Sven's escape. As a result, we were met by several interested parties. We visited the fisheries college on the island of Gossen where Sven was Principal. Convinced the Allies would invade the west coast of Norway, the Germans considered the island strategically important, and it was cleared of its inhabitants for an airfield. At the island's war museum, seated around a long table decorated with candles and lupins, we were offered fish soup, *smørbrød* (open sandwiches), and countless cups of tea. Our hosts, white-haired, tanned people with little English, had beautiful faces enlivened by a memory they had to share with us.

Outside, the west coast evening stretched long and late with a layering of blue-island silhouettes that reminded me of the Summer Isles.

Diminutive Selma Moldsvor stands before us in slacks and a white blouse, keeping us indoors with stories of wartime resistance, and singing in her tremulous 80-year-old voice. After breathy attempts at composure, her speech stutters and stops. She picks up a brown paper package and holds it out to Ellie who slips off the paper, turns with a gasp to her brother and sister.

'Pappa's shoes!' she says.

A murmur scuttles around the room and Selma's face crumples between a broad smile and tears as Ellie hugs her. A sob rocks up in my own chest, some undercurrent of loss and memory ambushing me. It's deep, and inarticulate. I'm ashamed of my former impatience.

The brown leather shoes are passed from hand to hand around the room. Their laces are knotted, the tongues lolling inside, and the leather cracked, lifting from its stitching. A hole has been forced through at the left big toe, as if that foot was larger, or perhaps lengthened by a dropped arch. 'Admiral' is spelt out on a sole worn glass-smooth, holes bubbling in V-shapes at the pressure points of ball and heel. They have been well worn – the shoes of a practical man. Shoes he was wearing when a German sergeant told him, 'You will be shot as a spy'.

Sven Sømme – 'Pappa' – has walked into the room.

Sven was active in the resistance movement. He organised intelligence, gleaning news from the BBC by illegal radio and circulating it to the coastal communities near his island home on Gossen.

'Were not these summer days of 1944 among the greatest days of the history of the world?' he wrote. 'When four-fifths of all peoples were united in fighting Hitlerism in order to secure the human rights of mankind? Would it ever happen again that all nations would unite like this, acting like one people against one mutual foe?'

Arrested for taking photographs of a torpedo station, he was on a ship at Åndalsnes ready to be taken to military headquarters at

Dombås for summary trial, when he slipped away from a sleeping Hungarian guard who had shown him considerable kindness, and disappeared into the hills with a loaf of bread under his arm.

From Åndalsnes, he skirted high land to the south of Isfjorden, dropping down again into the Erstad Valley. He aimed to find a way southeast through the mountains to the valley of Eikesdal from where he had already planned an escape route across the Dovre mountains and into neutral Sweden. Unsure of the way from the Erstad valley, he was helped by a small group of local people, including André, a young man of nineteen. Meanwhile the Germans were searching every house in Åndalsnes and had sent out soldiers and bloodhounds in all directions.

'You cannot cross the mountains in these shoes,' André said. 'Try my boots to see if they fit'.

Leather had all but disappeared during the Nazi occupation of Norway between 1940 and 45, and people wore paper shoes with wooden soles. Nevertheless, André offered up his brand new boots. And so Sven Sømme left his shoes behind. André later became Selma's brother-in-law, and the shoes passed into her hands. They were lovingly cared for, even rescued during a fire that destroyed her home ten years before our visit.

André's gift of boots and his guidance over the mountains to Eikesdal with two other competent climbers were the initial link in a generous chain that ushered Sven Sømme 200 kilometres through wild and isolated mountain country that was still snow-covered in June 1944. Travelling often under cover of night without a map, adequate clothing or food, he slept in the open or in deserted summer farms, and hid frequently for extended periods before he could continue safely. Valley and mountain, valley and mountain; helping hand to helping hand. This was the rhythm of his journey. He was aware of the personal risk his helpers took, reflecting the 'morale and true friendship between men that had not been destroyed by the German occupation'.

Sven's description of the initial climb up the Erstad precipice wasn't confident: 'No path could be seen any more, but from olden times people had found their way up here to the vast mountain ranges, shooting reindeer there and carrying meat and skins down the precipice to their farms in the valley below... We had to cross several small glaciers which were hanging on the mountainside. I did it with the feeling that any moment I might rush 1,200 feet to the bottom of the ravine...'

Sven's guides secreted him into the folds and corries of the terrain, and gave him a window-frame to carry so that if challenged he could claim to be going to work on a mountain hut.

When the party reached the top of the precipice and a plateau – a frozen landscape of mountain, lake and river – the lower valleys looked to him, 'like deep and narrow cuts made with an enormous knife'. They passed a hut beside a lake that was buried by snow, right over the chimney. He was travelling only a month earlier in the year than us, but that winter had seen momentous falls. Nevertheless, he felt safer once high in the mountains: 'No German soldier had ever set foot up here, nor was he likely ever to do so... The mountains were ours'.

The mountain story Selma has told, traversing both danger and safety, has fortified me for the journey. So does her homemade pea soup, flat-bread and cheese. Standing in the garden as we make our final preparations, she strokes my bare shoulder and chats to Ellie. I sense in her touch the assurance that what we are about to do is important.

Photos are taken, journalists' notebooks filled, and we repack luggage so that items we won't need for a night in a mountain hut can be transported by road to Eikesdal. I still know little of the plan but Sven's account of 'the precipice', and a dense band of contours I've seen on the map, have given me some concern about how we'll cope with the climb. A lean, tanned, grey-haired man with startling blue eyes keeps glancing at his watch and frowning at our delay. Then he's introduced as Oddmund Unhjem, our volunteer mountain guide for the first two days of the walk, and I immediately feel less worried.

Oddmund leads us up a shaley rock-strewn path under looming crags. We start to get the measure of our own fitness. Oliver, 6'5" and a ski instructor, lopes along comfortably. This is his first mountain adventure on foot, and his conversation is studded with exclamations of 'cool' and 'wicked'. Having lived and walked in Scotland for fourteen years, I'm surprised when he points to one of a succession of cairns, and says, 'Do you think these piles of stones are deliberately put here, to show the way?' He farts his way up the steep slope, laughing, exhilarated by the sound of his body working.

An arthritic knee keeps brother Bertie hobbling slightly at the back, but Oddmund allows us frequent stops. He tells us he's 73 years old, but it's hard to believe. We all breathe more heavily than he does.

Mist awaits us above, hanging and billowing in the notch of the precipice. A river throws itself down in a mighty waterfall, just as Sven described. Oddmund finds for us the hidden windings of the path between the crags. The story starts to come alive. And we take delight in finally using our bodies to retell it.

We climb out of the valley, and reach the plateau at 1,000 metres after only two and a half hours. The air is cool. Peaks and pinnacles tower over the turquoise waters of Gröttavatnet. We make ourselves at home in the hut which was buried under snow when Sven passed sixty years earlier, and cook up couscous and noodles.

The summer evening avoids nightfall like a child on holiday, a mist colluding with the sunset to drape the mountains with rose-pink blankets. A couple are celebrating their thirtieth wedding anniversary with a night in the hut. The light evening extends for so long that another couple who have joined them for a meal don't leave the hut until 10pm to walk back down to the valley.

Sven and the companions who guided the first part of his journey shouted, sang and called to each other as they walked across the plateau:

'Is this the right way to Stockholm?'

'Right, O, just turn left at the second set of traffic lights.'

He was clearly exhilarated, not just by the conviviality of the group, but by the scenery. He wrote about the view at the end of the plateau, just before the drop to Eikesdal, where 300 metre waterfalls dangled. Each side of the lake was, 'flanked by wild mountain scenery... The mountains grey and blue with greenish-white glaciers like collars around their necks...'

'I realised now,' he concluded, 'that it would have been madness to try to cross the mountain alone... First the Erstad precipice, then twenty-five miles across an unfamiliar mountain landscape, and then how would I have been able to find my way down the Eikesdal?'

They dropped down the steep side of the valley and then walked ten kilometres up to its head at Finset. The farmer, Nikolai Finset – whose Father, Kristian, Sven had met 24 years earlier – sheltered Sven in his house. Nikolai's ten-year old son, also named Kristian, was sworn to secrecy.

It's a bright, cloudless day when we leave the hut, clattering steeply down to the shores of Gröttavatnet through loose boulders, and 'skiing' on our boot soles where remaining snow allows. Bertie stumbles, slowed by his painful knee. As we wait for him, Oddmund expresses concern about our pace, considering the distance we still have to go that day, and about how Bertie will cope with the steep descent into Eikesdal. We each take some of the weight from his rucksack.

At the southern tip of the lake, we pick up the rough road that crosses a high plain of rock and shimmering snow. It's a long, hot stomp. Bertie's knee swells further. He limps. We wait. When an all-terrain vehicle chugs into sight about halfway across, he takes the offer of a lift. The rest of his time in Norway will be spent in the valleys. Close to the road where we wave him goodbye, a rotten timber frame has been cast aside, partially buried in long grass and we claim it as a physical remnant of Sven's story – the window-frame he carried to disguise the intention of his journey.

Finally we stand on the eastern edge of the plateau, just as Sven had done, looking down at Lake Eikesdal snaking a narrow mirror away from us between sheer slopes. This wild mountain country, this glorying in the heights, is what I've come for. My desk and computer seem remote and irrelevant.

We descend 1,000 metres, zig-zagging down the wall of rock through steep birch forest, wading through flowers, grabbing at blueberries as we pass, with sheep bells clanking around us, down to the green flat meadows and farms of the Eikesdal valley: a deep low groove cut into a high land.

We're met by Kristian Finset, the Kristian who as a boy had kept quiet about the man hiding in the spare bedroom. We're expecting to camp, but he offers us beds in his house. Kristian is a quiet man with a kind, round face. Following a stroke four years earlier, he's only gradually recovered his power of speech and doesn't know the place of things in his kitchen. His wife died from cancer just one month earlier, but his face broadens into a grin each time one of his grandchildren appear. Under his shirt cuffs, I notice the edge of a cream-coloured wool interlocked vest, the sort I wore at primary school and have never thought of since.

The next morning we are tourists – showering under the tallest waterfall in Europe, swimming in the lake, discovering *potatokake*. Our biggest worry is how to keep the chocolate from melting. Then we walk slowly up the valley towards Finset where Kristian's son, another Nikolai, gives us accommodation at the family farm. The walls inside the clapperboard house are cluttered with photographs of weddings, and a framed needlepoint for each new child, stitched by their grandmothers. Kristian shows us the room where his father had concealed Sven.

That evening we walk up into the blunt end of the valley to visit Kristian's daughter, Marit, in a turf-roofed timber house she and her husband have built. We sit in a garden backed by a sheer cliff. Her eighteen-month-old son powers across the lawn on all fours while the other children are scattered to the hills to fish or pick flowers amidst the same buildings and bridges that watched Sven pass.

Marit tells us about her job as a high-powered IT consultant, working from home. This arrangement seems to highlight the difference between rural life in Scotland and Norway. Human history and contemporary presence meet in this landscape – even the places most remote from urban influence may be inhabited. In Scotland such places are more often abandoned, remaining haunted by a sense of previous presence.

Below Nikolai's farmhouse the water sprinkler pulses and the river rushes all through the night. I watch dawn from the deck, looking back through interleaving slopes of the valley walls. They define, where they meet, the way we've come. The V of sky to the northwest never darkens. A thin mist settles in a kink of this valley that invisibly links members of the Finset family – Kristian, Nikolai, Marit – in a line of homesteads now gently ticking with sleep.

Sleepless myself, I imagine the Sømme family as a kind of valley that stretches back in time with parents, grandparents, stories, photos. It stretches ahead too, with children; cousins who become keen swimmers and ski instructors. And the valley intersects with others in this landscape of my insomniac creation; other family valleys with legacies running backwards and forwards through it in seams, connecting through the story of Sven's escape.

I observe the genetic legacy of the family who follow Sven, noting sulkily how as I am now 45 and childless, there will be no-one in the future to walk after me. Looking the other way, into their past, tickles up something like envy. Sven's children have found a way of bringing their father closer, memorialising him in a walk, and it's been made possible because a memory has been so vitally kept alive.

'If I ever grow up, shoot me,' Sven had apparently instructed his family. I wonder if my own father might have said something similar. I have no memory of him. He died of cancer in 1961, just as Sven did. Although he was a keen mountaineer, I know little of what and where he climbed. I have no scent or record of his adventures. For all I know, he might even have climbed here in Norway.

My own valley seems strangely punctuated. I'm inclined to think of myself as a full stop.

Before he left the Eikesdal valley, Sven copied a very rough map of his route onto a piece of sandwich paper. Nikolai supplied him with oats, butter, bread, pork, dried milk, a towel, soap, thread and a needle. Then he gave Sven a rucksack to carry it all in, and accompanied him out of the valley, up towards the elevated Lake Aursjøen.

Nikolai carried three heavy planks on his shoulder. It only became clear what these were for when they reached a narrow canyon down which a stream writhed. He laid them across the rocks from one side to the other to make a bridge. Sven's hands were seized in farewell, he crossed, and the planks were removed. He was alone with no retreat.

Sven worked his way along the lake-side, wading some of the streams and rivers cascading with melted snow, until he reached an unoccupied *seter* – or summer farm – at Gåsbue, where he slept the night. At the next *seter* a young man chopping logs told him that there had been Germans in the area, searching for a man escaped from Åndalsnes. A little later, he saw two men on the hillside, observing the area with field glasses. After that he walked by night.

He had passed the watershed dividing the east and west of Norway but now attempted a difficult crossing of a major and swollen river, getting drenched and cold, and having to retreat to avoid swimming. He had made it his habit to walk for two hours, lying down to sleep, then walking again to avoid hypothermia. Finally, walking upstream, he found a bridge over the river, and then he crossed the railway and main road between Oslo and Trondheim. Hares and their shadows were making a playground of the traffic-less night road.

The military headquarters at Dombås, where he would have been taken for trial, were to his west, and further Nazi installations to his east. But now he could look ahead to the Dovre and Rondane mountains and to arriving at his friends' at Lake Atnsjøen, which he estimated to be a further 80 kilometres.

Even now that he had the rucksack, he deliberately carried little, wanting to cover ground quickly. 'My principle was to carry just enough to survive and as light a burden as possible so as to be able to cover a great distance in a minimum amount of time.'

We've each bought a new rucksack for the trip and put too much into it. Ellie, Yuli and Oliver unload some unnecessary things to send home before we leave the farm at Finset. Kristian weighs each pack on his farm scales. Mine is heaviest at 18kg. It includes my own tent and stove, the trappings of independence in case I should leave the party and go off alone. It's an indication, I think, of my wavering commitment to the project when I set out. Now we no longer have assistance transporting our luggage, my hips and lower back begin their argument with the weight.

It's another of Kristian's sons, Viggo Finset, who accompanies us on the steep climb out of the valley. With sun smouldering on our shoulders and young birch flaring up the silver-grey rock, we climb until we can look down onto the roof of the farmhouse. The flat-bottomed, steep-walled Eikesdal valley stretches away, impossibly green. The river finds its wooded edges, first on one side, then the other, meandering in a pleasing line towards the Lake.

Viggo needs no planks to set us on our way. The stream runs dry since a hydro-electric project diverted it. But two generations on, the geography of Sven's escape still runs deep.

As we take the old path beyond the crossing point, scratching through juniper, blueberry and young birch towards a dam, I enjoy the sense of walking a storyline – a line that began for us with Sven's shoes. The goodwill offered to our own journey in memory of the original one seems remarkable. Although it's a story to which I thought I had no connection, I feel uplifted and claimed by it.

At the dam on Lake Aursjøen, Viggo leaves us to return to the farm. We are not able to follow Sven's route along the shores of the Lake because it has since been flooded for the hydro. Instead, we are pushed higher onto bleak moorland. We strike out for our first unassisted night, finding small patches of turf between the boulders on which to pitch our tents as dusk falls at ten-thirty.

Despite the great kindness of all our helpers and guides over the last days, I feel some excitement when we reduce to four – Ellie, Yuli, young Oliver and myself – and become truly independent.

We close in around the campfire, eating chocolate-covered marzipan and comparing blisters. With characteristic ingenuity, Yuli has protected her toes on the walk with small curls of fleece she brought from home. The effect of pressure and moisture has felted the wool into tiny socks, fashioned to the precise mould of her own toes. She has created artefacts of surprising beauty that we all admire.

When I first knew Yuli she was spinning and weaving, but more recently she's started to make felt, creating colourful and gorgeously textured fabrics which form hats, coats, wall hangings and even shrouds for green burials. Our creative lives have developed in parallel, both of us driven by them, seemingly unable to escape their demands. One of us creates fabric, the other text. I like the idea that our crafts are linked by an ancient metaphor. The capturing of stories onto written paper invoked the word 'textus' from Medieval Latin, meaning 'thing woven'.

We read aloud from Sven's book in the firelight and I think of the note Yuli wrote to me on the back of Map One, which we have now walked beyond. She said of her father's book: 'Do hope you enjoy it and get inspired. He (Sven-Pappa) was very much a man of his time. He was a hunter but after he fell in love with my Mum he became more of a shooter with the camera – my Mum's influence!' Yuli had wanted me to like him.

His words act as a touchstone now, a reminder of what was at stake, and they reinforce the meaning of our own walk. Because in some senses we are walking for pleasure, it's easy to forget how it would feel to be here alone, and in danger. We have good boots and equipment, no Nazis in pursuit, no need to travel in the night.

Despite his discomfort and fear, joy frequently surfaces in his account, buoying him with a sense of tremendous freedom: 'I had escaped torture, imprisonment and death, I was free like the birds singing around me. There was no school any more, no more responsibility, no property to take care of. Life was ahead of me. I was an outlaw.'

Sven's love of the mountains, his holidays spent skiing, swimming, fishing and hunting, had given him a thorough knowledge of the land. To reach the high passes without leaving a scent that hounds might trace, he waded up burns. In order not to leave tracks across patches of snow, he bent the tops of supple young trees down to the ground and then used the resulting 180 degree 'flick' as a means of pole-vaulting to the other side.

His love of his country, its people and its nature clearly sustained him. He heard a Scottish accent in the scolding rattle of the ptarmigan: 'rack-gack-gack-garrr'. His spirits rose as he watched a herd of reindeer gallop through a bog, becoming lost in the spray of water and moss that rose from their hooves.

We enjoy reading of experiences we've shared with him already: red squirrels trapezing through branches; golden plovers making their plaintive call, 'tleee', and running fitfully towards us. Like him we've grazed on blueberries and wood sorrel in the forests. In marshy areas, we've picked cloudberries whose taste Sven characterised as 'sunshine'.

I sleep better in the familiarity of my tent. Rain patters on the flysheet in the night, but when I get up in the morning, it's dry and the clouds are parting. I wash myself in the small pool we're camped beside. Every time we pass such places, Oliver asks enthusiastically,

'Do you think there are fish in there?' But I meet none. We brew coffee and prepare ourselves for the day's walk towards Dombås, unsure how far we'll get.

The path crosses a featureless plateau, and circles behind a small hill, after which we descend back towards the Lake through rocky outcrops and the welcome embrace of young, green birch. We spread out, each falling into the step of our own world. There are views along the twenty-kilometre length of the Lake, and we arrive at a cluster of tourist cabins at Gåsbue where we meet a small road, and therefore, people. We cook up tea and some vege-burger mix, and realise how tired we are. Not much further along the lakeside road, we make our next camping stop amidst a band of carnivorous mosquitoes.

Oliver wakes up the next morning disenchanted with the journey – he has been bitten all over and is starving. The remaining rations are low, and are very unappealing to him. After we set off, he walks a long way ahead of us. When we reach a campsite where we hope to find a shop, it's closed. We tough out a long, hot stretch of road from the end of Lake Aursjøen towards Dombås discussing our food fantasies. Chicken, lemon curd, apple juice and roast potatoes are Ellie's. Yuli, Ellie and myself blast out an African greeting song to sustain our steps, and Oliver hides his head in embarrassment when a group of cyclists approach.

The second campsite has no shop. Depression begins to brood around us. It's still over 10 kilometres to Dombås. Just when we most need cheering, a couple in a camper van give us juice-rich apples. When they offer us a lift to Dombås, we take it.

Soon we're eating pizza and cake in a café and watching people go by, noting the temperature climbing to 34 degrees now that we are sunk in a valley and on tarmac. I prod at the sore spots ground into muscles around my pelvis by the weight of my pack.

Oliver, demoralised, and with other priorities, decides to leave us here and go home despite wanting to support his mother and honour his grandfather on this journey. We all feel the loss of his youthful energy, but it's hardest for Ellie as we wave him off from the railway station the next morning. I wonder how it will feel now to be three. We award ourselves a rest day and spread out the remaining maps for a planning session.

I have with me a small metal map-measuring wheel. It's the only one of my possessions I believe to have originally belonged to my father. We run it along the lines made by Sven Sømme's feet, measuring the distance. I enjoy using the wheel for this but am also pricked by something like sadness. As if the feeling is locked under ice or seen through smoke; I'm not quite able to identify it.

I show Yuli and Ellie how to estimate the time each section of the walk will take with the slowing effect of ascent taken into account, as per Naismith's Rule. We research the location of shops to replenish food stocks, and decide on a stopping place for every night. The map becomes less abstract; the journey is now constructed in our imaginations to its end.

After the freezing river and the speeding hares, Sven found a valley to follow south-east into the Dovre hills, hoping that it would lead to a mountain pass and over to the Grimsdal valley. It was difficult in the dark, traversing a series of steep ravines slippery with frozen snow. He found himself at 1,500 metres above sea level, following a line of cairns that poked through snow and mist across an endless-seeming plain.

On this bleak, high crossing, he sank into an emotional crevasse. He saw a pair of lapwings – the male sitting on a stone and the female running between boulders – noted that they were far from their usual coastal area, but felt nothing. 'My heart was numb', he wrote. Marching hour after hour along the cairns he thought of his family and friends, the Germans, his narrow escape, and could provoke no strong response. He worried: 'Would that feeling last after I had returned to normal life?'

But the landscape lifted him again as he began a gentle descent, down amongst birch woods, juniper, open meadows. Finally he could see a rough road winding beside a shallow river that ran to the south-east, with the Rondane Peaks rising beyond. Below him was a group of *seters,* a tourist hut, cows and goats grazing.

'There was no doubt that this was the Grimsdal valley. I had arrived where I was hoping to be'.

A short taxi ride out of Dombås rejoins us to Sven's route just after his river crossing. We walk from Fokstugu across the Dovre hills, climbing steadily onto a plateau bleakly reminiscent of the Cairngorms. Grey shale has been shunted about by thousand-year-old glaciers and speckled with yellow lichen. It rains.

Ellie looks about and shivers. 'He was so exposed,' she says. 'Imagine how invisible a grey Nazi uniform would be here; how easily a small figure moving alone could be picked off by a sniper.'

But when we look closely, we find the grey desert mocked by miniature 'gardens' – cushions of bright pink moss campion, fluorescent green mosses, and alpine anemones, Sven's favourite flower.

'They belong to the mountains,' he wrote, 'where in early spring the first snowless patches appear. They peep up from the ground, pudgy buds, clad in a fur coat of grey, silken hair...They are the flowers of freedom.'

He was confident the German soldiers would never see this flower, or him, so anxious were they to stick to what they called 'civilisation'.

On a shaley hill, climbing out of the last dry glaciated riverbed in the Dovre hills, I stumble. I pitch forward down the slope. And at some point, hands out, I realise I am going right down, not recovering my feet. My shin strikes something. Then 18kg of rucksack follows gravity, hits the back of my head and cracks my face onto rocks.

'You look pale,' a voice.

I put on a fleece.

'Your nose is crooked,' says Yuli.

Blood drips from somewhere. My forehead. Shaking and shock.

There are one and a half hours still to go to the Grimsdal hut. I find a compacted lump of last winter's snow, and walk with it pressed to my forehead.

During the walk, the arrival at the hut, the tent going up, and my attempts to emulate normality by eating waffles, cream and strawberry jam in the hut's cafe, purple fluid swells into bags at the corners of my eyes. My brow feels top-heavy.

'I'll be fine if I rest,' I tell the others, thinking of our plan for the days ahead; afraid of my first ever night in a hospital.

But Yuli shakes her head. 'I really think you should have it seen to.' A friend of hers had a head injury when they were on a cycling holiday together, and she is all too aware of the dangers.

My new boots are scuffed and sun-worn, and we are about half way along the route to Sweden. I've walked for six days, just got my rhythm, and finally found myself on good terms with my pack.

Tears come for the second time in the trip as Yuli and Ellie smile sadly, waving me off in a taxi to rumble down the track to the nearest village doctor. I look back at the V-shaped groove which has beckoned for the next day, the entrance to the Rondane range, regarded as the finest alpine hiking country in Norway and an inspiration to many Norwegian writers. I am not sure whether I'll be back.

Rather than treating me and returning me to Yuli and Ellie as I hoped, the doctor dispatches me into the night. I travel south in another taxi to Gjøvik and hospital, with a driver nodding at the wheel after his full day at work as a butcher. We aquaplane on mountain roads transformed into rivers by a sudden storm. Lightning fills the 2 am sky. My driver tells me he has travelled the world as Norway's number one boogie-woogie dancer, but now would like to be a rally-driver, to experience the thrill of sliding, almost losing control. I fight sleep during the three hours our journey takes and try to keep him talking.

Perhaps aware of my fears, he sees me into the hospital. A woman gives me a pair of pyjamas and a bed, and looks after me as if I'm the hospital's only patient.

'We try our best', she says when I comment on her kindness.

She wakes me in the morning, asking, 'Did you manage to sleep at all?'

I feel my way into all the sore places I hadn't noticed before – stiffness in my left arm, a cut under my watchstrap.

But when I see the consultant he tells me that my nose is too swollen to be treated now; I have to fly home.

By 9.30am I'm discharged, an Elephant Woman straining to see the world beyond my own face because of the swelling across the bridge of my nose.

Then I'm walking alone around Lillehammer, sitting in an internet café booking an early flight home, waiting for a bus. A woman and her child look at my bruises in momentary horror. When the woman makes eyes contact, she looks away. The child does not. I see other people reacting in such ways. Perhaps it seems that I've invited a beating.

The reminder of the biting hills rises all around me as I travel back up the country to retrieve my belongings. I am in Peer Gynt country; I am following an ancient pilgrims' route that should be calling my feet; I am hazed and estranged. I sleep in a motel below Grimsdal, dream of my mother, waking at each revisit of the fall with my hands fluttering out to save me.

The motel manager knocks on my door in the morning.

'No headaches?' he asks, seemingly pleased that I'm still alive.

I find a telephone box, pump in coins on a call to my sister to tell her what's happened. Standing on the brink of self-pity and tears, I fight to stay on its landward side.

Although many people turn away from the trouble they seem to read in my face, there are still strangers who help me with arrangements for my pack to be brought down from the mountains. A checkout girl in the supermarket near my motel picks up the telephone to the hut warden. Her father arrives smiling with it at the supermarket.

Then I turn south again. As I arrive off the bus in Oslo at midnight, a prostitute outside a nightclub is the only person who stares directly into my face and asks, 'Have you had an accident?' It's as if we share an underworld.

I leave Oslo on an early morning flight.

Thankfully, Sven did better than I did.

Not long after Grimsdal where I left the route, he arrived at Nesset, a farm he knew well, belonging to the Norwegian Academy of Science. His friend Hjalmar and sister Inga who lived there didn't recognise him at first in his lean and ragged state, but helped him to hide out for several weeks in a tent above Lake Atnsjøen, while waiting for the safest moment to head for Sweden. From here he managed to make contact with his wife, saw his brother Knud, fished, watched otters and divers, and was treated to food and rest while he re-planned a route and enlisted the help of friends to cross some major rivers to his east. Along with a false passport and ration cards, he received a message written in invisible ink. People of his home district of Romsdal were overjoyed that he'd out-witted the nine hundred German soldiers sent to recapture him.

Then he pressed on east, travelling through dense forest, crossing rivers and lakes and increasingly marshy land, making contact as he did so with the helpers pre-arranged by his brother. Sven met a man late one night, and they stopped to chat 'as wanderers used to do when they met in the mountains'. He knew to trust the man when he offered him a cigarette.

'I see you are the right person', the man said, finding that a piece of paper inside the packet matched his own. He then led Sven to the river.

The most dangerous part of his journey ended with a knock on the door of a Swedish farmhouse, 'the door into freedom'. He became one of over 48,000 Norwegians who walked or sailed to safety.

After Sweden, he came to Britain in September 1944 to join the Norwegian Ministry of Agriculture, returning to liberated Norway in

1945 in King Haakon's convoy escorted by the British Navy. He gave each of his helpers a watch engraved 'in grateful thanks for your help in 1944'. They are still shown off by descendants today.

In the days following my fall, I pictured Yuli and Ellie, the remaining journeyers, small figures in a high, wide landscape. They were well equipped, confident and determined. Although I was sorry not to be with them, I was proud to have been part of their journey. Like Sven, they rested up at Nesset. They found their father's signature in the visitor's book and met Hjalmar's widow. Then they pressed on through wolf and bear country, the bogs and rivers, to finish just short of the border into Sweden two and a half weeks after setting out.

Their steps had reinforced their father's route, but they had also worn their own pathways of personal meaning. For Ellie it was a way of experiencing a little of the effort the journey had cost him, and a means of reclaiming Norway as a country to which she belonged. For Yuli it was a kind of route finding towards her father. But it was also political, a response to a new climate of war following the invasion of Iraq the previous year.

Reaching their final campsite at Engerdal, they lit eight candles for the river to carry. There was one for each of us who'd set out on the current journey, one each for their mother and father, and one for the Hungarian guard on the ship at Åndalsnes who they learnt was shot for the carelessness which allowed Sven to escape, and saved his life.

As dusk fell, they watched eight small lights float down the river in remembrance of a man whose funeral in 1961 they were deemed too young to attend. Then in celebration of a journey, they ceremoniously burnt the socks that had both cushioned their feet and chafed up blisters.

Sven's story remains marked with its own memory-stones, as clear as a white-pebbled path visible in the dark. Like the best folk tale or legend, it has been passed on and then on again. Sven may have avoided leaving prints in the snow for his trackers to find, but he left lasting markers in people's minds and in their concept of the landscape.

I set out on this walk principally for a holiday, but it came to mean much more. I discovered a richly peopled landscape. Even in the strangeness of the days following my accident, the generosity of strangers playing their part contributed to a sense of a living, resonant pathway.

I returned home thinking about this. I felt the need to follow more whispering ways; to seek out stories that still echo underfoot. And I began to wonder if that could include a faint path with a strong personal connection.

I started asking questions, and I acquired a photo. Summer 1952 in the Swiss Alps. A young man, slim and fit, stands with hands on hips in front of a pine tree. He has a cravat around his neck and a face that, although shaded by a squint-brimmed hat, hints at features like my own. He looked so alive here with his hemp rope, canvas rucksack, rolled up shirt sleeves, wearing a grin – yet 8½ years later he was dead. I began to wonder if I could identify one of his journeys, or even a route he had ambitions for, and walk a memorial to him.

But I doubted I could do it. It might mean a climbing expedition in the Alps, a formidable challenge that I had never tackled, and I no longer trusted my own feet.

Outlasting our Tracks

Fiescherhorn
4048
Agassizhorn
3946
Finsteraarhorn
4273
Grünhorn
4043
Fiescher
Glacier
Finsteraarhorn Hut
KONKORDIAPLATZ
Hollandia hut
Konkordia Hut
Grünhorn lücke
Lötschenlücke
Lötschental Valley
Aletsch
Glacier
Eggishorn
2926
NORTH

Finsteraarhorn,
Bernese Oberland,
Switzerland

..the wonderful and terrible things that happen in high places...
Gertrude Bell

A single electronic note by my ear stands me upright at 3.45 am. I tiptoe towards the others in their dark bunks, and Colin raises a hand. I understand immediately that he's been awake for hours – in the last ten days the three of us have named ourselves the 'Insomniac Mountaineering Society'. But Rick's shoulder needs a shake, a whisper to pull him from a dream.

Rick had greeted the previous morning sardonically: 'I didn't expect to see spindrift on my summer holidays'. Mutinous winds and blizzards blasted us over the Grünhornlücke pass towards the Finsteraarhorn Hut later in the day. Through the Hut's huge windows we then watched cloud-shadows dance along the summits of the white range opposite. The conditions had sent us to bed questioning the viability of today's climb.

A glance through the window now reveals a miracle: Stars. A skyful of them. Colin has told us the rule his father had in the Alps – if you can see five stars, you go for it. There's no discussion. Rick brings to the breakfast table the news that not only is the sky clear but the wind has stilled. There's a sense of a charmed day emerging. The few other climbers at the hut, are as alert to the promise as we are.

Alpine huts before dawn are brutal places. The air of the crowded boot room thickens with the sound of zip-pulling, plastic rustling, the thud of heavy boots on wooden boards, the clunk of ice-axes. Climbing harnesses jangle with metal hardware as they're strapped tight. Our efficiency is tripped up by apprehension, things not to forget, lack of space. No-one makes eye contact.

By 4.45am we're jolting our bodies into life with a scramble up the steep rocks behind the hut. The blue and white markers painted amongst the shelves and chimneys that make up our path, lurch up late in the head-torch beams. My lungs feel pinched by 3,000 metres of altitude and by my pack pressing from behind. As ever it's heavier than it should be.

Above a crest of rock we meet the ruins of the old hut and take a ridge northwards. At the boundary between rock and snow our silhouettes congregate with those of ten Italians going for the same summit. They are hard-muscled, fit-looking and a lot younger than us (collectively 150 years).

A cry goes up from Rick as first sun pricks pink the Fiescherhorn and Grünhorn peaks. During the minutes in which we put on crampons and rope up for the snow-field ahead, an illuminated pink curtain drops down the snow-covered mountain wall opposite towards a murky chasm. Later in the morning, it will bleach to white and stretch down in jaggy fingers, prising aside the dark walls of the valley to flood the Fiescher glacier with sunlight.

The ritual of roping up has become familiar over the last week and is oddly comforting now. I find the rope's mid-point and fix it with a clove hitch onto the karabiner on the loop of my harness. Then I coil spare rope tightly over my left shoulder, and tie it off to my harness in a knot. After the fumblings and uncertainties of the previous week when we were acclimatising and practising all this on climbs in the Arolla area, the tying of the knot is now almost automatic. Finally I wind a prussic loop between the rope that will run ahead of me and the karabiner. This will be vital if I fall into a crevasse.

A line of shared responsibility now snakes between us, demanding to be watched so that our distances can be adjusted for different conditions – slack or taut, depending. The rope makes a team of us, summoning us out of individual reveries and slow waking with the need to communicate. Like riding a tandem, pauses will need negotiation.

We move off slowly, no head torches needed now. Colin leads, finding a line towards a rib of rock that descends from the summit. It's high above us, but we'll level with it at a place known as the Frühstückplatz or 'breakfast place'. I follow, always between the other two, taking least responsibility. Between Colin's mumbling and Rick's deafness, my role sometimes seems to be to shout messages fore and aft – 'Crevasse ahead!' or 'Happy with the pace?' or 'Should we be going higher?'

By covering the footprints of climbers in the days before us, the new snow has made pioneers of us, erasing the accepted route, forcing us to be slow. It disguises crevasses and snow bridges, laying itself in soft piles that our first laborious steps sink into and compress. Those behind us will harden it into an easier-going trail. We would prefer not to be leading.

It's here on the first snow slope, as we take a line that puts us ahead of the Italian group, that my mind spools away for a few minutes, to focus somewhere inside myself. As if it's a revelation, comes the thought: 'I'm climbing the Finsteraarhorn'.

Finsteraarhorn arches its back north-south through Switzerland's Bernese Oberland. The Canton's highest mountain had been summoning Rick and Colin for many years, and they had finally chosen it to celebrate their fiftieth birthdays in 2008, twenty-five years after they first climbed together in the Alps. By coincidence, this mountain still chimed faintly in the memories kept alive by my family.

After the Sømme walk in Norway, I'd asked questions about my father's mountaineering. I wanted to colour in the shaded outline in his photograph, to have some stories to walk or tell. It must have been from him that I inherited the 'mountain gene', but how little else I seemed to know.

When I asked for specifics of mountains or routes, it was only Finsteraarhorn that could still be named. My mother pointed at its daunting profile in a brown leather album. A fine sheer fin rose up. Massive ramps of rock piled one on the next to make up its western slopes. My sister shivered when she looked at it. At half my age, in 1952, my father led his own expedition here.

If I was to answer the call to follow him, I reasoned to myself, I had to start my Alpine climbing career before I reached fifty. I thought at first it would mean joining a commercial expedition, something I always resist. But when I talked about it to Rick – an old friend who I've walked and skied with in Scotland – he and Colin agreed to absorb me into their trip, bravely, considering my inexperience in the Alps.

I sought out books, looked up the position and the terrain on Google Earth, and then opened the 1:25 000 map that bears the mountain's name. It's the only sheet in the 247 of the Swiss Survey series on which not a single surfaced road is marked. A tiny area of green appears in the top left hand corner where the land drops down towards Lauterbrunnen.

I put the map flat on the floor, but it refused to lay low. Grey hatched ridges were linked by tight contours, conjuring high, wrinkled, remote land. Pale blue glaciers coursed across it, five of them radiating out from a central point named Konkordiaplatz after the busy Paris interchange of Place de la Concorde. Another glacier system writhed its way up the right hand side of the paper, towards Finsteraarhorn. But Konkordiaplatz, resembling a huge ice-hydra, spread its tentacles as if forcing the mountains apart, to occupy the majority, the centre, of the map.

My father's party must have reached Konkordiaplatz by climbing out of the long green valley of Lötschental. My sister and I holidayed there in 2003, wading through flowers on the valley sides below the snow-sealed peaks. We gazed at the steep and coruscated glacier below the Lötschenlucke pass with the relief of those who know they're not called to it. In fact I'm sure we believed it to close the valley in rather than provide a route beyond. We had no idea then of our family connection to the valley.

A wrinkle in geography and time had Rick and his family staying in a village just up-valley from us. Colin joined him the following week, just after the death of his own father with whom he'd climbed, skied, scrambled all over these mountains. It's almost as if we were unknowingly then staking the ground for this trip.

Gaining height clarifies geography and has always been one of my reasons for mountaineering. You link up what have seemed like separate, dead-end valleys in patterns which have little relationship to what you understand when travelling by road or rail. I sensed our respective journeys – my father's, Colin and Rick's, my sister's and my own – spreading from that meeting place of deep ice.

Studying the map tickled up in me a sense of magic, but it was magic tinged with fear. It hinted at a world quite beyond my known territory from which I might emerge enchanted, altered. Or terrorised.

To reach Konkordiaplatz we had walked up the hydra's southern tentacle – the Aletsch Glacier. At 23 kilometres, it's the longest in the Alps. We dropped into a steep valley just under the Eggishorn until a cliff of ice towered a shadow over us. Then we climbed a feature I've learnt to call the *bergschrund* – the mysterious and potentially dangerous boundary between two worlds, where rock and certainty disappear under a lip of ice.

I'd seen photos of the glacier taken from the hills above; a two kilometre-wide swathe carving north-south between a corridor of high peaks like a massive bubbling river, its tail flicking south-west to narrow and melt towards the Rhone. The curves of its long slow valley-ward journey are emphasised by two dark veins of medial moraine, trapped by ice pressing in from both sides.

We abandoned rock at the dripping lip of ice. There was an anxious scuffle over the unstable edge where warm rock was melting it. And then came the first splintering-loud steps onto the glacier's back as it levelled out. Starting out on our journey northwards, I looked up and ahead. I could see nothing but the immediate surface. The ancient body was wrapped in dense fog.

Disorientated, I felt I was walking on a sea that had been struck still at a moment of monumental swell. For the first hour my steps were diffident. The ice gleamed up a dull grey where gravel had been trapped in visible pockets. Score lines were etched across it in great arcs. It was a troubled surface, holding secrets under scars and curved scratches, burping up occasional groans from beneath our boots. Crevasses yawned, drawing my eye down into twisted interiors that were sooty black or turquoise and shelved incrementally towards inconceivable depths. Stalactite teeth leered out at me. The ridges between crevasses rose and fell; great whalebacks and miniature mountain ranges which forced us to divert to find places where we could jump. Colin was a misty sub-marine silhouette, disappearing into a distance that was impossible to judge.

This wasn't a walk of rhythm and thought, but a strict regime of care and concentration; watching for the route, avoiding the catch of a crampon on an opposite gaiter. I felt I was in a faded black and white movie, haunted by the image of Frankenstein and his monster wandering fog-drunk on the ice. Where algae had coloured old snow, tinting it pink, it lay in fat slabs against the monochrome, incongruous as steaks. The glacier crept at its own pace that had no need to engage with the human world, or explain itself, shaping the land around it as it went.

I thought of Scotland, its familiar valleys defined long ago by creatures such as this; valleys whose shape and residues still hold the mark and memory of ice. As John Ruskin said: 'the footmark, so to speak, of a glacier is just as easily recognizable as the trail of any well-known animal,' allowing us to imagine the seas of ice which once engulfed such landscapes.

The surface was tamed in time under my crampon claws. I gained confidence, but I longed to see the dark hills on either side that defined our corridor. How would we know, I wondered, wandering in this labyrinth of fog and crevasse, when we were level with the high rock to our right on which perched the Konkordia Hut where we would sleep that night? Might we not walk right past it?

I glimpsed the dark seam of medial moraine carving before us. Then the wide sweep of Konkordiaplatz dropped below the mist curtain ahead, promising, with a white glow beyond the far lip of fog, the rise of further glaciers, further peaks.

It was then that a photo my father had taken came into my mind.

The three in the photo – Jim Parry, Effie Pendleton, and David Lawton – are blurred in black and white, paused with backs to the camera. Standing on the glacier that's carrying them in from the south-west to where their route will meet ours at the Konkordiaplatz, a hemp rope connects the three to my father, the photographer. They stare ahead, away from him. Finsteraarhorn peaks high in the furthest eastern distance and I imagine that's what they're focussing on. It's as if the glacier has stilled the flicker of their feet on the deep snow, forcing them to listen to its wisdom sighing beneath them, their lives a tick-tock in its long slow voyage.

The trail after my father has been slow. As a child, I remember searching for photographs, trying to find proof of his existence to fill the gap of memory. In the stiff second drawer of the dining room desk I stole glimpses, framed and pasted into albums.

In preparation for this trip, I wrote to The Alpine Club, believing my father to have been a member. I ferreted in the memories of my mother, my uncle, a former girlfriend of my father's. A few more details emerged, and the brown leather album revealed its trail of black and white photographs and postcards. The dark hills and skies of the Lake District were there, the cat Bulan perched on my father's shoulder outside my parents' first home. There were picnics on Devon clifftops with my mother, father and his mother and father. My sister as a baby.

And my grandparents' house and neat-lawned garden at Earl Richard's Road, Exeter. I remember my grandfather sending me to collect snails from his borders of snapdragons and michaelmas daisies, and ending their destructive trails by dropping them into the water butt.

The week before he crossed the Konkordiaplatz, my father went, like us, to Arolla. He was with a party from the Oxford University Mountaineering Club (OUMC), climbing in the ranges that spike up from Val d'Hérens. The first pages of the album hold photos of this trip. They feature young tanned men with tangled hair, holding up wooden-shafted ice axes as they pose for shots when the going is easy. Names of people and places are scribbled on the reverse side of the photos in pencil. Two or three hands argue on some of them:

'Looking south from Petit Mont Collon?'

'No. But I'm not sure what.'

'Boquetis ridge?'

'Yes. That's it I think.'

In his postcard home of 23rd July he described their first day in Arolla – 'We were up at 5.15 this morning to do the climb up to and along the ridge shown [la Petite Dent de Veisivi] ...Maybe part due to altitude we thought we couldn't make it, but did and had [a] wonderful view of Matterhorn and Dent Blanche. On ice for first time tomorrow.'

When I contacted the Oxford club, they were able to help with the Arolla part of the trip. The Journal of that year contained an account – the climb of Petit Mont Collon, traverse of the Dent Sud de Bertol, a blizzard on the Pigne d'Arolla, a retreat from the summit of L'Eveque caused by unstable new snow on top of ice, a traverse of Mont Blanc de Cheilon including the Arête Jenkins, and so on. The record had Rick remarking: 'Wow, they really went for it, eh?' And I felt a prickle of pride.

'Dick' his fellow climbers called him. I've grown up without a name for him, lost as he was to me before I had much language. I imagine him as the life and soul of the party at the campsite in Arolla, and at the Hotel Collon where they drank local wine and ate *raclette* and got thick heads at a birthday celebration. I imagine him speaking French in the huts. Perhaps, with his musical ear, he was responsible for his party, 'making feeble and tuneless responses to the gay and lovely songs of a party of Swiss', as recorded in the club journal, while they basked in the sun on Tête Blanche on the last day of the club meet. As I read the joyous words of joint adventure recorded in the OUMC Journal, Richard Cracknell, the summit-hunter began to materialise.

The Club had no record of the trip to the Bernese Oberland the following week; it was clearly an informal arrangement with two other Club members. They were also joined by Effie Pendleton, another Oxford student who was the fiancée of David Lawton. Family folk memory says my father was worried by having her along, as she was less experienced and might hold them up.

The pencil scribbles helped me trace their journey – Hollandia Hut, Konkordiaplatz. There were several postcards of Finsteraarhorn with words written on the back which fill in some of the story. Photos of the spiny ridge of the Finsteraarhorn were taken from the summit of Agassizhorn, just to its north. The photos seemed to stop there and I puzzled over how the climb of Agassizhorn related to their ascent of Finsteraarhorn. Did they return to the Finsteraarhorn Hut for a night before climbing it? Or climb the entire ridge from the north, meeting our route at the Hugisattel, now just rounding out of sight above us? Is that what had made them so late in the day? I remained puzzled, but just accepted that it would make more sense once I had experienced the lay of the land myself.

I imagined my father, in this three weeks or so of adventure before his 'grown-up' life began, feeling viscerally alive as he breathed in fine Alpine air. He was 25 years of age in 1952, and had just finished his Chemistry degree at Oxford. He would have been disappointed that his final year's research on longevity was disqualified because the source of his studies had been discredited, but he had a job to go to with ICI in Middlesbrough. He was an accomplished enough mountaineer to be leading his own party, and had been involved in the equipment tests for the first successful Everest expedition, which he and my mother would hear news of from the Lake District the following year.

His mountain photographs feature equipment made of canvas, wool and hemp. When I prepared myself by looking at a few websites about alpine climbing gear, I was quite overwhelmed by recommendations for lightweight crampons, clothing made from Windstopper, Polartec Powershield, Schoeller Dryskin Extreme, etc. I decided to make do with a 20 year-old ice axe, borrowed crampons, wool leggings under summer-weight walking trousers.

If you listen with eyes closed as rucksacks are organised the night before a climb, there are two predominant sounds – the trill of zips being pulled and the rustle of plastic bags. My father didn't have the benefit of a plastic bag when he came to the Alps. It was not long afterwards, however, that he started to work with epoxy resins which were then a whole new chemistry, and probably brought him into contact with carcinogens. His interest in longevity was a cruel irony – a terminal cancer killed him only eight and a half years later.

As we climb the pristine snow slope towards the rocky ridge that holds the Frühstückplatz, we become aware of a muffled line drawn right to left across our way. In several places it gapes open, reveals the crinkled edges of a crevasse; the nearer we get to it, the more cavernous.

'Don't like that,' says Rick of the suggestion we cross it to our left where it reaches towards a rock spur falling steeply away into the valley.

A wide snow bridge is directly ahead of us, dipping slightly between two open mouths. Aware of the tricksy appearance of this new snow, we creep towards it a few steps at a time, as if approaching a dangerous animal that might suddenly charge us. We look up at the third option – a circuitous high route to the right which arcs into a strong-looking bridge over the crevasse. Then we focus ahead, aware of the risk we're taking.

Colin coils slack rope in his hand while behind him Rick and I stand firm, ice axe picks turned outwards, ready to brace on the ground should the surface fail him. Then he's down on all fours, scuffling across the crevasse with the rope swinging and pads of snow kicking up behind him, climbing up onto safer ground. When he's upright, it's my turn.

The snow sucks at my feet, and I'm floundering with both arms and legs as I ride the back of the deep, struggling for breath. If the snow bridge gave now, I'd surrender with relief, stop fighting upwards and sink into the depths to be free of gravity, and regain my breath.

When we are all three across and able to view the yawn of the mountain below us, we signal to the Italians to take the higher, less direct route, thus condemning ourselves to be the leading party for most of the remaining climb.

Soon we're clunking crampons onto the stone rib, climbing to the ledge of the Frühstückplatz, where we do as the name suggests, eat chocolate, and gaze at the dawn-lit mountains rising to our west in peaks and spires. The Fiescher glacier slinks through its shadowy rock corridor below us, a silent turbulent river.

We don't linger long, gripped as we are in a cold west-facing dawn. We look up to the shaded snow slope steepening above a gnarly area of crevasses. This slope defines our next two hours of ascent up to the Hugisatell, the saddle from which the more technical part of the climb begins.

The warden at the Finsteraarhorn Hut has warned us that it's on the steep slope looming above us now that there are sometimes difficulties after a fall of snow. It could be uneven – heavily collected in some areas and thin in others. The angle, especially higher up, could spell avalanche trouble. Yesterday this suggestion had me shivering with apprehension. Today I feel differently.

It was Franz Josef Hugi, a natural scientist from Solothurn, who declared, 'The very ascent of the Finsteraarhorn... is absolutely impossible for human beings'. Admittedly he was speaking about a different route, but on August 10th 1829 with his guides from the Hasli Valley, Jakob Leuthold and Johann Währen, he explored the route we, and most other climbers, take today via the south-west flank and north-west ridge. Because he sprained his ankle, the guides were forced to leave Hugi behind a little above the 4,088 metre saddle, while they continued to make the first ascent of this monarch of mountains. The saddle was later named after Hugi.

Edward Whymper, a legendary figure of early Alpine mountaineering, was the first to climb the Matterhorn on his eighth attempt. Four were killed in the descent, leading Queen Victoria to ask if mountain climbing shouldn't be against the law. Whymper understood risk as the crux of mountaineering, and following the accident wrote a reflection which is often quoted as advice: 'Climb if you will, but remember that courage and strength are nought without prudence, and that a momentary negligence may destroy the happiness of a lifetime. Do nothing in haste; look well to each step; and from the beginning think what may be the end.'

On our relatively short journey from the Konkordia Hut the day before, I felt my resolve falter, beaten down by spindrift-sharpened winds reminiscent of the worst day on a Scottish winter hill. As we plodded towards the Grünhornlücke, Rick's cheerful voice sprang up behind me.

'There's the sun.'

Disbelieving, I looked up and saw a pale misty disc. At regular intervals, he then gauged the unveiling:

'Sun – two out of ten.'

'Sun – six out of ten, and you've got a shadow, Linda.'

'And there's Finsteraarhorn,' he said as we arrived at the col and looked ahead where the mountain should be. A wall of fog had performed on it a vanishing act.

At each step down the other side and particularly once on the snow-disguised ice platform of the Fiescher Glacier, I expected the surface to subside and plummet one of us deep inside. Each of us sank a leg into a crevasse; it was a matter of time. I began to question the taking of risks, the necessity of going higher, exposing ourselves to avalanche danger. Not for the first time, I asked why I'd imposed this ordeal upon myself. The questions that had accumulated on pre-departure sleepless nights passed again in a chain, hand over hand. Will I be fit enough? Will I manage the knots and ropes? Will I suffer from the altitude? Will I be afraid?

A chorus of these doubts whispered just behind me as we approached the Finsteraarhorn Hut. I was finding enough adventure and commitment in the blizzard-scoured journey to this interior without climbing any higher.

'I'm not sure I'm up to it,' I had finally said.

But now the snow slope climbing to the Hugisatell above us looks even and firm. There is no wind, and sun is promised. All is less forbidding; hope, not fear predominates; height beckons. The trudge begins.

The pace is crucial. Seemingly ludicrously slow, it has to allow us to keep going for two hours without over-heating and so exhausting ourselves. Zips can be adjusted but with a harness on and roped up, clothing changes are impossible. Efficiency with time in Alpine climbing can be the difference between life and death. It's essential to descend before the surface deteriorates to slush, snow bridges weaken, banks of unstable snow succumb to gravity and avalanche. Faffing is for the Hut.

Colin, as ever, sets the perfect pace. But as ever I wish I was fitter. Although I'm never truly unfit, I've not had long days in the hills for some time, and my training at home was curtailed two weeks before departure by a fall down the stairs which cracked my ribs. I'd wondered at the time if my body was colluding with the night-whispers to sabotage my trip.

And so goes on the mesmerising trudge towards the Hugisatell, a time of breath and foot coordination, punctuated by the squeak and groan of the ice axe penetrating frozen snow. I'm charmed by the precise, crisp line of delicate claws we tattoo onto the snow, like hermit crabs' scuttled trails across white sand.

I plant the ice axe; lift my left foot through; lift my right leg through. Plant ice axe, and repeat; and repeat. Every motion is deliberate, and moon-walk slow. On slightly less steep ground, I can increase the pace by planting the axe simultaneously with one of my feet so it's a two-time rather than a three-time rhythm. On even easier ground, the spike of the axe simply trails in the snow. But that easier ground is not here.

Under the helmet brim my glacier-goggled eyes stay keen on the purple rope flicking and twisting bright against the snow ahead. I try to keep it taut enough to prevent it catching in Colin's crampons; loose enough to prevent irritating tugs on his harness. Plant, one, two. Plant, one, two. I rarely look ahead, only to discourage myself with false summits.

'The Finsteraarhorn,' I think again. 'I'm climbing it.'

First sun slinks over the saddle to our side of the mountain, and up ahead Colin's red and yellow fleece roars into a blaze. The babbling line of Italians approach behind us as we pause for photos.

'I have three young men, very strong,' their leader says to us, coming level. 'I think they can go ahead now.'

The string of three march past us, silenced by effort, carving a serpentine way around final crevasses towards the golden-glossed snow scoop of the Hugisatell. As I look towards the rock ridge to its right, a gilded line flashes up against blue sky, holds briefly and then dies over our side of the ridge – a tight whirlpool of illuminated spindrift, suggesting that our relative warmth and shelter may be short-lived once out from the lee of the mountain.

We arrive on the corniced brink where the mountainside falls away at our feet, throwing up ahead of us all the peaks previously hidden to the east. A gnarled head of ice and rock spars up to our right where we will go next.

I learnt at the Hut that Gertrude Bell, famous as an Arabist, had made the first attempt on the northeast ridge of Finsteraarhorn in 1902. She rarely makes an appearance amongst the lists of men in Alpine climbing histories but her account of the ordeal in a letter to her father is terrifying in its detail.

'The arête... rises from the glacier in a great series of gendarmes and towers, set at such an angle on the steep face of the mountain that you wonder how they can stand at all...' Her party climbed onto the arête, 'beyond the reach of the stones the mountain had fired at us (fortunately with rather a bad aim)...', but were eventually forced to retreat, from a position within view of the summit, with 'snow blowing down the couloir in a small avalanche'.

The descent was as dangerous as the failed ascent. Amidst blizzard and mist, her ice axe was teased by lightning, which provoked her cool words: 'It's not nice to carry a private lightning conductor in your hand in the thick of a thunderstorm'. She spent the night in a tiny crack with a guide sitting on her feet to keep them warm, and continued back down the arête the next day, shivering in continuous snowfall but resolute: '...when things are as bad as ever they can be you cease to mind them much. You set your teeth and battle with the fates.'

Having reached the relative safety of the Unteraar Glacier, damp matches failed to ignite, even under the tent of her skirts, and they were forced to spend another night out, huddled against the elements, making the full expedition 57 hours. Her climbing partners later applauded her courage and endurance and her reminders to keep eating. On safe arrival at Meiringen, she consumed a great many boiled eggs and jugs of hot milk and discovered her toes to be frostbitten. This made Finsteraarhorn the last cry of her extraordinary climbing career.

Perhaps it's the dichotomy of elation and terror that draws us to the knife-edge, but also what keeps people away. I'm puzzled by the lack of women participating in such adventures today. A rough head-count at the huts revealed one woman in ten, a proportion represented in the Italian party now stamping their feet next to us. Maybe it's that women look for more meditative experiences in the mountains; suffer less summit fixation. My introduction to Alpine climbing the previous week certainly had me wondering if summit fever was for me. There was something absurd in the convergence of scant-breathed people on coffee table sized summits, when great sweeps of undulating ridge, glacier and col remained spread around us, pristine and unoccupied. It brought to mind John Ruskin's scathing attack on climbers and tourists despoiling the Alps in his lecture *Sesame and Lilies* of 1864: 'The Alps themselves, which your own poets used to love so reverently, you look upon as soaped poles in a bear-garden, which you set yourselves to climb, and slide down again, with "shrieks of delight"'.

On the bus up the Val d'Hérens towards Arolla at the beginning of the trip, I'd looked longingly at green meadows, the dark weathered wood of the ship-strong houses, verges effervescing with flowers as they fell behind us. I'd had my head in a hay meadow near one of our campsites, and a cricket had whirred the clover and grass into a thrill of life. All the long walk up to the monochrome heights of Cabane de Dix, marmots whistled us through the valleys and we named the small yellow fields of pasque flowers, the quintessentially alpine gentian, alpine clover, huge bright violets.

Is this alpinism really 'me', I wondered? Don't I prefer the lower ways and passes where lives still linger, where green things grow; not these heights which above 3,000 metres seem equally to belong to any Gore-Tex-armoured warrior who gets there first? If this is Alpinism, am I really equipped to deal with its fearful implications? I began to think that the lure of the summits must be a young person's game, something that my father never had the chance to outgrow.

On one of our rest days between Arolla and the Bernese Oberland we'd met a woman who told us two climbers had been 'lost' from Cabane de Dix, just after we left. Sitting in valley sunshine about to eat fresh apricots and cinnamon buns, I'd been quite stunned by this news, as if their lives had brushed against ours before they died. I imagined being at the hut when guides brought the bodies down, the sobering of the mood, and the arrival of a sudden starker sense of danger.

I wondered why Effie Pendleton joined my father's party in 1952.

The only woman. Was it to prove that she could, out of a love of high places, or simply to be in the mountains with her fiancé? I like the look of her from the one photo in which she faces the camera – a compact body that looks strong, balanced; layers of clothing peeled back for exertion; a high bounce of short dark hair, and under her goggles, an easy smile. Her hands pause in dark mittens at her sides. She looks comfortable in this environment, ready for adventure.

I've studied the guide book and know the words almost by heart, clinging to the ones that imply easiness – the grade, *facile*; 'scramble' rather than 'climb'. I know that the route first traverses the western flank and then moves onto the ridge itself. Way up above us, I see the snow crests and cornices leading up the ridge until blunt rock thrusts skywards in greasy-looking blocks. No-one has been up it since this fall of snow, and it's whiter now than any of the photos I've seen.

Illuminated snowflakes float between me and the bright jackets and smiling faces of the re-assembled Italian party. They continue to stamp their feet, and have put on their windproof layers. We put on ours, re-coil the rope around our shoulders, eat chocolate. I start to feel cold. Someone has to go first.

At 9am, a little more than four hours above the hut, amongst peaks in three countries stretching up to kiss the sky, and with the Italians continuing to prevaricate, we lead on.

To reach the ridge requires an awkward haul up a short, snow-silled crag. Colin pulls himself up, and fixes a belay to secure my ascent. My crampons are insecure and slippy on rock, arms too weak for the necessary push-up. The longer I flounder, the louder rises the chorus from the Italian audience behind me. Then I'm up, quickly followed by Rick, and we're moving on the loose, unmarked snow that's accumulated on the slope.

Each step is hard-earned. Colin slashes the adze of his axe into snow until he connects with something hard – rock, older snow, ice – to which crampons will cling. Before I stretch a foot up to each step, I empty it again of the soft showerings that Colin's next cutting has sent down. I spear my pick as hard as possible into the slope to my left, seeking purchase in ice or around a rock so that a secure foothold is backed up by a hand-rail. The glove on the axe is sucked deep into soft snow, and is soon wet and freezing to the shaft.

'Remember to stand upright,' Rick calls. 'Don't hug the hill.'

And he's right. To have weight on the crampons, one needs to be perpendicular to the hill, but it feels like leaning out. I don't look down, or think of the potential slide. I look for rocks over which I can loop Rick's rope behind me, a small pivot point between us should one of us slip – probably an illusory security. I look at what's immediately ahead.

It's steep and slow, but I can breathe, my moves feel strong, and we are undoubtedly heading for the summit. A glance over my shoulder reveals the Italian hard-men, miniaturised on the Hugisatell, sitting in a sunlit pool of red coats far below, watching our progress. The glance also reveals a pair of climbers gaining on us. A beard, a pair of rectangular spectacles. New faces. We greet and agree they should pass us. Colin is tiring from all the step-cutting, and they're faster than us.

Gertrude Bell said she could recall every part of the north-east ridge, and I'm similarly gripped by the features I turn to for support, and try to trust. There is an absolute focus which knocks away any other thought, image, even a glance at the extraordinary views. There's just a faint sense of the falling away of any other land around us, our penetration into the sky, as we climb the highest in the Bernese Oberland. I barely ponder the distance to the summit, just keep an eye on the pair ahead of us, concentrate on the security of each shift in my body, the sympathy of the rope ahead to Colin.

As we move towards the crest, rock begins to burst through the snow flank. Colin points out here and there a flake to grip, something to allow the body a strong swing around an upward-jutting boulder. I know that this mountain is infamous for rock falls and that in general the risk is increasing with climate change, but I shut out the thought.

The crest is messy – jutting rock followed by corniced soft snow, a sudden shocking gulf of sky beyond it. Each step on the crest spreads a revelation of new geography; steep slopes rising in range after range below and beyond, should one dare look. We are walking in the air. Each further step is a bonus. I have no sense of time. But Colin has paused ahead.

'What are you thinking, Colin?' I ask his back.

There's a long silence. Then, 'I'm knackered.'

We can see the pair ahead have climbed up onto a prominent block, are having a drink and assessing their way ahead. There seems to be some levelling out – we can't see beyond it, and I wonder if we're nearing the summit. We pause, waiting to see what they'll do next.

'We're going to turn back,' a Czech voice calls to us.

'Yes,' says Rick behind me, as if they're confirming his own thoughts.

'There's much snow before the summit,' comes the call again. 'It will take perhaps another hour and a half. And we're concerned at the condition of the snow for the return.'

With the turn of the day, the planet, we see that the sun is now stroking the south-west face of the mountain down which we must return – warming, melting, creating hazards. An approaching tide.

None of us argue.

We move up towards the snow crest, cut a small platform on which we can perch three abreast, crampons bracing us from the drop below, so that the faster pair can pass us. Sitting close, we tame our movements to avoid dislodging each other, tease chocolate out of pockets into mouths, drink and exchange words, eyes levelling on the mountains to our west.

The Czechs begin their descent, bodies turned upright into the mountain, moving together, traversing towards us. Ice axes splutter up snow flurries, the surface a swell and fall under them. Then the men descend steeply, directly below us. I see how difficult this is going to be. Our journey is only half way complete.

I hear a bee buzz close to my ear, an incongruous reminder of the valley, hours and days below us. When will we be back again amongst flowers, crickets, bees?

'The only thing that matters,' says Rick as we set off again after the Czechs, 'is getting down safely. Take your time.' An echo of Whymper: 'Do nothing in haste. Look well to each step...'

And I feel almost overwhelmed with gratitude for this permission. It calms me, and with Colin below me suggesting holds for my hands and feet, I slowly re-find the steps of our ascent, backwards. We see that the Czech climbers, having reached the Hugisatell and rejoined a third waiting there, are watching us down the steep snow flank. They get up and leave just as Colin says to me, 'You can turn outwards here', and we begin again to do something that resembles walking – become upright figures with two-time legs, arms dropping by our sides. Even the flounder-crag seems easier on descent.

Our feet touch down onto the safe-seeming, smooth snow of the Hugisatell. When we look at watches, we see that the ridge has gripped our minds and bodies for four hours. This is what Rick calls 'mental fasting', the absolute focus of mountaineering that clears all else. Now it releases us to a group hug and photos. Words flow again. We have the mountain to ourselves, and sit in a colourful row, laughing, spreading slabs of bread onto the 'table' of Rick's knees to layer with cheese and squirt with mayonnaise from a tube. We revel in a sense of achievement, but mostly just in the joy of being up here with, 'one crowded hour of glorious life,' as Whymper (quoting Walter Scott) would have it on finally reaching the summit of the Matterhorn.

Colin points north west. 'The Eiger!'

We look along the continuation of the ridge we're on. Beyond the conical white peak of the Aggasizhorn where my father stood to take photographs of Finsteraarhorn, we see the dark grey flat-topped mountain that Colin has picked out.

We spin through 360 degrees. Colin and Rick name the peaks that years of familiarity with geography, shape, and distance have made theirs. In most areas of Scotland I can do this – know hills from different angles by their relation to each other and to lochs and valleys, despite their shape-shifting. Here I'm still lost, although the characteristic shapes of the Matterhorn and Mont Blanc have followed us around enough now to be landmarks. The dark rift of the snowless Rhone Valley separates us from the further reaches of the Valais and last week's mountains, now looking remote and white.

'How many days do you get like this in a lifetime?' asks Colin. 'Perhaps thirty? If you're lucky.'

I've walked alone so much that it strikes me suddenly this sharing is what mountaineering is about. I feel incredibly lucky to have walked the last days fastened in trust to these two men, while following my father's footsteps.

Perhaps it's this that overcomes all the absurdities of what we're doing – that mountaineering, going to the heights, keeps us young in spirit. And, as Whymper said of his scrambles in the Alps, he was repaid for his toil by two of the best things a man can have – 'health and friends'.

A bee settles next to my hand on the snow, buzzing, bright and fuzzy with heat; the valley calling.

Four hours is half an office day, a long match at Wimbledon, a short night's sleep. How had it seemed like half an hour we were on the ridge? This landscape of ice and rock seems to have exposed the elasticity of time, contracting it in some odd way relative to the primeval heartbeat of the mountains and their slow-moving glaciers.

My father, because he was just that, has always seemed older than me. Yet he came here at half my age. The postcard he sent to his parents shows Finsteraarhorn, sharp-spiked, seen from Grindelwald. But it carries a wretched rather than a triumphant message:

'11th August 1952

Gasthof Restaurant Glacier

Grindelwald

to Mr and Mrs Cracknell, 11 Earl Richard's Road North, Exeter, Devon, Angleterre

'Dear Mum and Dad, I am very cross that you have been told about this miserable business before I have had a chance to let you know myself... I have just got down from showing the guides where the body lay... This is what happened. We had almost finished our journey, we were roped and traversing a difficult ice fall to one side + we stopped to put on crampons to cross a steep ice slope. Three were together on a small rock and I at the back on the mass of the rock. Suddenly I saw a large boulder falling clear of the slope and shouted. The girl was standing and did not duck quick enough and the back of her head was smashed and she died at once. Jim panicked + David was personally concerned so I got them out of the way, removed rope + gear from her and secured her to an ice axe and then led them off over difficult and dangerous ice to the hut, arriving after dark. I volunteered to stay for the guides. I look forward to home. Tell Jenny in case papers garble. Love Richard'.

In an extra note he added: 'incident at very top left of photo'. I've studied the picture on the postcard again and again. His description suggests the near vertical eastern side of the ridge. I tried to convince myself before the climb that it must be a trick of perspective, re-reading his note to try and find a different meaning, a different location from that high, haunting spear of mountain. I'm still puzzled how his party came to be so high up so late in the day. But none of that matters now, and it seems there is no-one left to tell me.

In the same photo album, amongst the postcards and photos, is fastened the reason for the family memory of the mountain's name, a small stark press clipping:

'STONE KILLS A GIRL CLIMBER

10,000 ft Up Mountain

Grindelwald, Bernese Oberland, Sunday –

Mountain guides today carried down Miss Effie Pendleton, 24, an Oxford student killed by a falling stone 10,000ft up the Finsteraarhorn. – Reuter.'

I wonder if it came to haunt him – this place, the 'miserable business' that befell him here. Gertrude Bell pokes two fingers in my ribs – one for 'terrible', one for 'wonderful', for they are both here with my father and myself, juxtaposed. I wonder if my joy now can mend that dark twist in history.

This mammoth ridge that towers over and arcs through the Bernese Oberland, must have represented my father's threshold into adulthood. As he descended the mountain for the second time, with guides carrying Effie Pendleton's body, he was setting out on a longer journey, well beyond the mountain hut – to the green valleys, to Exeter and parents, to Middlesbrough to take up his first job as an industrial chemist for ICI making the pink plastic 'gums' into which false teeth are fixed. He would be engaged to my mother in less than six months, married and starting a family by 1954. Finsteraarhorn was his last venture into high places.

He and my mother moved to the Netherlands with my brother and sister for his job with Royal Dutch/Shell in 1958, where I was born the following year. From there we took family holidays in the green Austin van with a square ventilator in the roof that's one of my earliest memories. On reaching the Austrian Alps, we no doubt kept him low in the valleys, and I imagine him throwing occasional glances to the snow-peaks, and thinking of a time, when we were older, when he might climb again, and perhaps introduce us to the high places.

Rick is beginning to do this with his fearless eight-year-old son. I imagine them coming to the Alps soon, a garrulous pair, with matching smiles and long legs and their affinity for rock and heights. The manager of the mountain shop in Fiesch told us that it would soon be the fiftieth anniversary of his first ascent of Finsteraarhorn, made at eight years of age with his father. Such markers of the years, celebrations of age and youth pulse though family memory. My father had all that to look forward to as I weighed on his back in the Austrian Alps, a wordless cargo. Apparently he carried me to the edge of a glacier, just to see it, and to marvel.

I think of the slow digging of a platform in the snow, the necessary anchoring of the body, and the marking of the spot. A distraught fiancé to bring to safety. How quickly my father must have had to grow up. The youthful alpine-aired faces in the photos from Arolla just two weeks before, turn away from the camera towards serious responsibilities, jobs and death.

As we revel on the Hugisatell, the only reliable thing about time seems to be the point in the day's turning – the sun is full on our route down and branding the skin of our exposed faces with reflected fire.

We descend the long, slushy slope to the hut, playfully when it allows – a glissading, rope-tugged bum slide – and seriously when sun-softened snow bridges have to be negotiated over crevasses. My face throbs where the insistent running of my nose has allowed the sun to pierce Factor 40 cream. Fiescherhorn and Gross Grünhorn grow higher and spikier ahead of us, polarised black and white as we sink lower. The unpredictable terrain of previous steps retrodden and shuffled into a mess of hard and soft now undermines our balance. I am unstable and lurching, rhythm-less, tugging taut the rope. Massive snowballs form on the base of my crampons and I jig along to my newly learnt tap dance with the ice axe dislodging them at each alternate step.

We gain rock above the hut with relief, un-pincer feet from crampons, cast off the rope to make ourselves independent people again, turn our faces at last away from the scouring heat. We scramble down the rocks that were in darkness when we came up at dawn. My legs still feel surprisingly strong and sure. Our return is heralded by the scavenging choughs.

Twelve hours after our departure we find the Hut transformed. The flags hang limp, the storm-swept wooden deck is now lined with drying boots and climbing gear. Dozens of T-shirted people brought from all directions by fine weather and firming snow are bathing in the afternoon glacier-light that we quickly retreat from, indoors. Amongst the buzz of beer drinking, the anticipation for many of the next day's climb, the Italian group is diminished by the new throng. They applaud our return. We catch at the eyes of two faces that feature a beard and a pair of rectangular spectacles and then burst into smiles. We drink a litre of sweet tea each and apple juice, too high to feel tired or sunburnt or sore-legged.

'I'm looking forward to seeing a tree,' says Colin, as if each day of our exile in this enchanted black and white world has been a year.

None of the three of us seems to feel that we failed to climb the mountain.

The next day we return over the Grünhornlücke Pass. The slim, pioneer trail that we made two days earlier has now been broadened by successive parties. Where we had been presented by a wall of fog on our journey here, we now turn to see the full west face of the Finsteraarhorn.

High above the Frühstückplatz, where the climbable slope rises under the sheer face of the summit ridge, the wisdom of our decision to turn back has been spelt out. A chaotic scribble of avalanched snow now partially covers the curved line of our footprints. We pause for a long while in the morning sun while we contemplate this.

Two strings of climbers appear from the direction of Konkordiaplatz to our west, their faces kissed into smiles by the levelling ground and sudden rise of Finsteraarhorn ahead of them. Rather as I imagine might happen in a chance meeting of hunters, they seek out our experience, asking about directions and conditions; part as colleague, part competitor. Then they move on, summit-hungry.

Unroping, we step out onto the slow deep sea of the Konkordiaplatz, the junction of streams of time. An eight hundred metre depth of ice moves in invisible increments under our feet. Like a tree and its rings, or a cross-section of coral that reveals growth bands through centuries, the glacier archives events of weather, and perhaps of human travel.

A little removed by the creep of the glacier lies my father's way across here. I wonder how far downstream the imprints of his feet have drifted in 56 years, try to imagine their changed patina, perhaps transformed into something resembling a fossilised leaf.

Whilst standing on this great sweep of a meeting place, my mobile phone signal returns for the first time in two days. I send home a message of reassurance; history has not repeated itself like the crossing of a dark rope.

I am warmed by midday sun, the Aletsch glacier is rumbling and gurgling off into the far distance ready to carry us downhill. In a matter of weeks the superficial imprints of the journey – bruised shins, sunburnt lips – will have healed. But I know this experience will echo on. A spell has been untied; a story retraced and given words out of silence.

Postscript: September 08

A reply comes from The Alpine Club in London. My father was never a member. But they do have a press clipping about the accident that I haven't yet seen. They kindly send it on.

I read:

'WOMAN STUDENT KILLED

GENEVA, Aug 10

Four English Alpinists climbing to the Finsteraarjoch (10,925 ft) on Friday were making for the Strahlegg Hut (8,858 ft) when they were overtaken by an avalanche of stones. One, Miss E R Pendleton, of Oxford, a student, was struck and killed. The others, who were unhurt, went for help. A party of eight guides from Grindelwald made an eight-hour ascent to recover the body, which late last night was brought down to the village.'

I look again at the map to try and make sense of this additional detail of geography. The Finsteraarjoch is northeast of the summit of Agassizhorn; the Strahlegg Hut further north-east still. This implies they were descending when the accident happened, and not descending from Finsteraarhorn but from Agassizhorn. 'Our journey was nearly over', suddenly makes more sense. They were heading for the valley, on their way to Grindelwald to the north-west. I look again at the postcard: 'incident at very top left of photo'. Below the high sharp spear of the iconic mountain I see for the first time a lower lump, further left. It would have been on their descent route. I am swept to a new conclusion.

My father clearly admired Finsteraarhorn, but didn't climb it. He chose instead a pleasing southwest to northeast traverse that probably took four or five days across the entire dramatic sweep of the Bernese Oberland, denying the enigmatic lure of its highest peak except as a sight along the way.

I'd been distracted by the spear of mountain and overlooked its lower foothills; saw my father as forever youthful, striving for the highest summits. In this way, his memory beguiled me into a climb far more challenging than I would have chosen myself. After my initial dismay at 'doing the wrong mountain', I've come to see it as his joke on me.

I also see how unreliable memory is, and how buried it becomes. My detective trails were slow and mazed, but it makes sense now that it was on Konkordiaplatz, rather than on the high mountain, that I felt the draw of our affinity; our common journeys. Somewhere on the slow glacier the plates of ice we've each trodden ground against each other, and our paths coincided.

The Heaven Above And The Road Below

Château de Lavigny, Switzerland, August 2012

I succumbed today to the call of the high places, took a day off from my desk at the Château and a series of trains east into the Valais, climbing in a tiny mountain tram up out of mist into sunshine, through forest and perched villages, passing glacial grey water in the rivers, toothy mountain views.

'I'm in the Alps!' my body kept shouting.

I walked up from the village of Les Diablerets through deep clover, crocuses, chirping crickets, up to the grazing at Isenau where I stopped to drink coffee on a terrace and gaze at the glacier above. I relished the cool air and sense of elevation at 1800 metres, but pondered how much higher I had been on the back of Finsteraarhorn.

Cowbells donged earthily nearby. It will soon be time for the cattle and sheep to be brought down from the *alpage*, the high grazing where they've been since Spring. Transhumance in the Alps dates back to the 4th Millennium BC. Unlike Scotland, where it was the women and children who accompanied animals to the summer sheilings, here a few herdsmen go, leaving the majority of the community in the valleys. It delights me that this traditional practice lives on, and that the animals make their slow walk home garlanded with bright flowers.

Today was a day walk, a loop. I resisted the lure of well-marked trails leading the eye towards lengthier possibilities. It's a joy, though, that's hard to beat: setting out on a long walk, the agenda for forthcoming days dictated solely by the beckoning road. The landscape unrolls, fitness grows, and even the slight sense of hardship and rationed food is enjoyable. Only taking what one can carry brings the ultimate sense of independence. As Robert Louis Stevenson said of his crossing of the Cévennes in 1878: '...the great affair is to move; to feel the needs and hitches of life a little more nearly; to get down off this feather bed of civilisation, and to find the globe granite underfoot and strewn with cutting flints'.

On a long walk in remote terrain life becomes simplified into a line, daily rituals, the rhythm of day and night. Added to this, a passage through a mountain landscape is punctuated by dramatic geographical features; passes and rivers to cross, junctions, inns and settlements, each of which can gather symbolic significance in a mind channelled by motion and perhaps solitude. In Scotland, I've become fascinated by old ways that wind through the hills; routes of pedestrian and animal travel where traces of human culture survive. I imagine myself a character in the literatures of long, slow journeys – Hardy's *Tess*, Christian from *Pilgrim's Progress*, Bilbo Baggins.

A palimpsest of footfall characterises the two walks that follow; a layering that the rhythms of my own tread seems to mesh with. Descending from the high places of the Alps, to foothills, passes, valleys in Scotland, and taken over a number of consecutive days, each is in my mind a 'proper' journey. But something else made them particular: both routes thrum with animal hooves, arousing in me a sense of the primal and migratory, an earthy and tangible link with the past.

The first journey is close to home, cutting across the southwestern Cairngorms amidst the pageant of a large group of walkers, in a landscape transformed by the new experience of travelling with pack ponies.

The second is an old drove road whose history has long fascinated me, but where the hoofs are hushed and ghostly. I walked mostly alone with time to reflect, delving into the deep litter of memory as I considered the way ahead. My route started from home and linked familiar places, but this was only revealed to have a purpose once I was in motion. Perhaps a subconscious drive made its way down to my feet and played a reverie out in steps and miles, helping me to mine some lost parts of myself and dwell on them along the way.

Walking links places and so creates continuity; places occurring both in physical and inner landscapes. We discover ourselves as we discover the world. Perhaps reclaiming our own stories through a physical act can help ensure that life's momentum doesn't take us sleepwalking onwards, shedding memories carelessly along the way. We may even walk ourselves into a whole new geography. In an age in which our major life changes are mostly unmarked, a long walk can fulfil a necessary ritual.

The Return of Hoof Beats

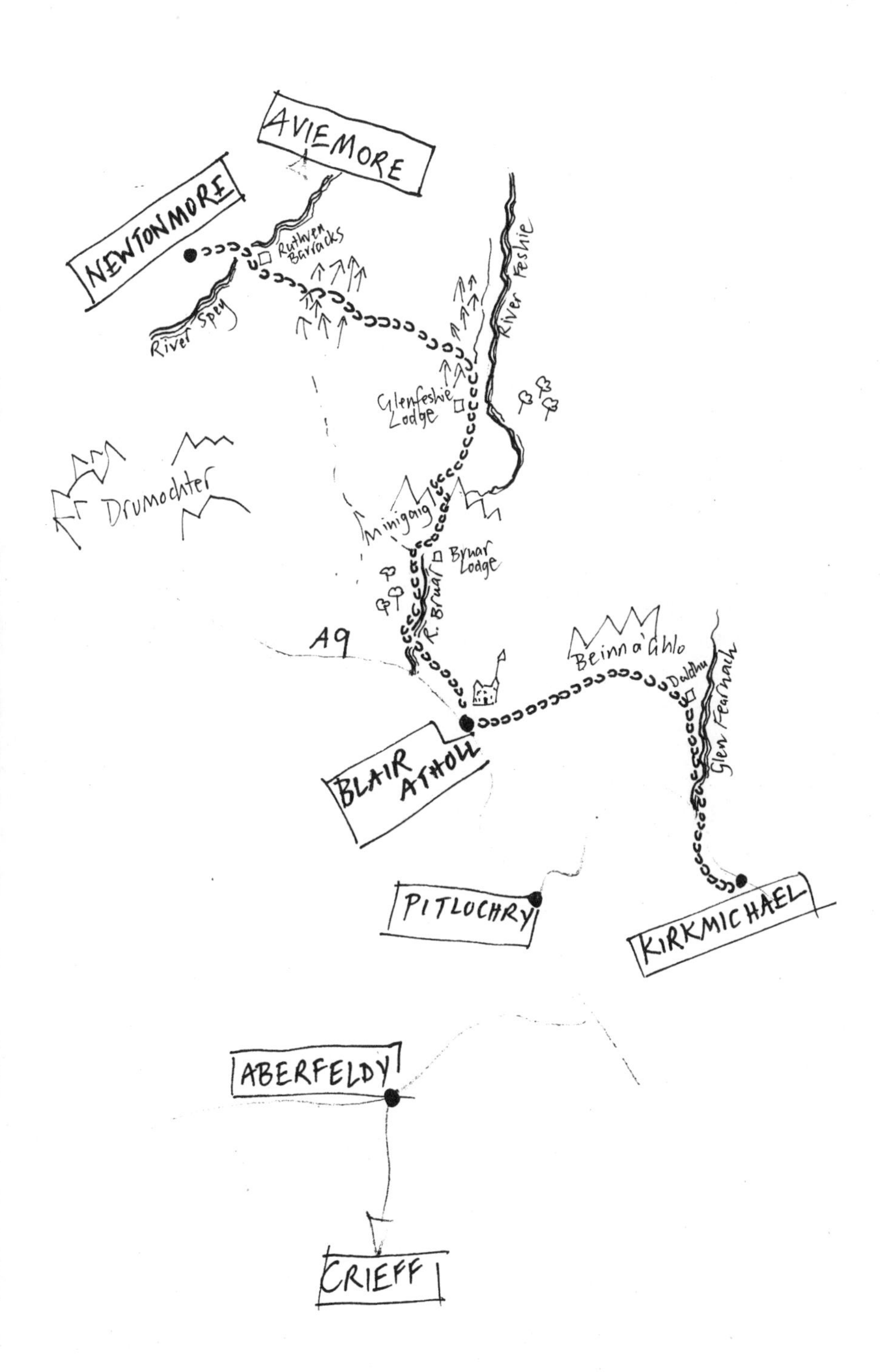
AVIEMORE
NEWTONMORE
Ruthven Barracks
River Spey
River Feshie
Glenfeshie Lodge
Drumochter
Minigaig
Bruar Lodge
R. Bruar
A9
Beinn a'Ghlo
Daldhu
Glen Fearnach
BLAIR ATHOLL
PITLOCHRY
KIRKMICHAEL
ABERFELDY
CRIEFF

Newtonmore to Kirkmichael, Cairngorms, Scotland

Travel ye moorland, travel ye townland
Travel ye gently far and wide
From *The Herding Rune from South Uist*

Ailsa – one of three youngsters gaining know-how as a pack pony by taking a journey with more experienced animals – careered away from the first river crossing, knocking her leader to the ground. As a local ghillie, he was well used to handling large animals and yet even he could be left winded and bruised. Our light-hearted chatter quietened for a while at this reminder that travelling with our luggage on a pony rather than on our backs, wouldn't necessarily be easier.

The opportunity to be part of this movement of people and animals over six days had prickled in me a half-realised dream. On a cycling holiday in Provence in 1996, a pastoral scene unfolded on a tiny road high in the hills. An old Datsun van was parked by the roadside with an orange flashing light and a large hand-painted sign on its roof, reading: *attention troupeau.* At least 100 sheep were grazing on a wide grass verge near two small tents. Two large shaggy dogs lumbered over to sniff and greet us. We found the drovers seated around a long table that in my memory is loaded for lunch with wine, cheese, salad, bread. The image conjured Thomas Hardy stories, rustic traditions that feel lost in Britain. It was October so perhaps the animals were being brought down to lower ground for the winter. I scented the ritual of a seasonal journey.

Our modest body of people and animals moving as one across an ancient-feeling landscape in Scotland was an 'unnecessary' journey but felt connected to a stream of time and a legacy of working journeys with animals. I'd envisaged it being a bit like a medieval pilgrimage; a flock of us grouping and regrouping as we moved, stories told along the way, and more created.

We travelled at a drover's pace of 10-12 miles a day using old ways and passes which once forged lively connections between places. From the Highland Folk Museum in Newtonmore we turned away from the Spey's north easterly trajectory and travelled east and then southeast. The statuesque landscape we entered seems 'wild' now because of its remoteness from most human traffic and habitation. It's relatively unmarked physically by the web of seasonal trails that would once have kept it busy.

Days one to three took us between Newtonmore and Blair Atholl, places now more usually linked by a fifty-minute drive along the A9 looping to our west. In order to join a good track through the upper reaches of Glen Feshie to another in Glen Bruar, we had to cross the high hills that rise between them. This crossing would take us to the Minigaig Pass, the summit of a once important north-south road. With a three mile plateau at 2,500 feet, it was not favoured in winter and was known as the 'summer road to Ruthven'. It may sometimes have been used by drovers from Speyside taking their cattle to market in Crieff or Falkirk via Glen Bruar. But after 1729 when General Wade built his military road over Drumochter – further west and now under the A9 – the Minigaig way became popular with drovers as a way of avoiding the payment of tolls.

A hard look at the map in advance should have shown me that the unconventional linking of routes would be the crux of the journey where the challenges of pony handling and navigation would be greatest. But someone else had planned the route; someone else was responsible for the ponies. Carried away by my childhood pony romance and a migratory journey, I avoided the detail.

In 2000, Joyce Gilbert, a 'networking entrepreneur' in the field of outdoor learning, organised a journey to be shared by 20 people of differing disciplines -- ecologists, outdoor instructors, poets, artists, educators. We set off in Canadian canoes from Ruthven Barracks near to the source of the Spey River and followed it (ever faster, ever wetter) to the sea over five days.

Twelve years later we set off not far from the same point. Of the 25 or so of us aged between 15 and 63 who travelled at least part of the current journey, only four of us had been on the original Spey trip, but the cocktail of backgrounds was similar. At our communal heart lay a fascination with journey and the urge to discover a sense of place. There were also individual motivations such as a wish to walk with animals, explore and draw creative inspiration from the landscape, follow old ways and keep traditions alive.

Few amongst us had much experience of ponies except for two long-distance riding enthusiasts including Vyv Wood-Gee. Inspired by the history of droving and its massive impact economically, socially and environmentally, she had already walked and ridden drove roads in different parts of Britain. In 2010 she took eight weeks with two sturdy black Fell ponies, Micky and Magic, to follow in drovers' footsteps 900 miles between Dunvegan on the Isle of Skye and Smithfield Market in London. She observed the relics of trysts and stances and ways through the land where traces remained. With no support team, she carried all she needed, riding one pony and using the other as a pack animal, and enjoying the growing bond between them through hardship and hospitality. Fortunately she ate better than the drovers who had survived on oatmeal and onions and occasionally on blood drawn from their cattle.

The history of droving in Scotland had inspired all of us. In its heyday from the mid 17th century, drovers from all over the north of Scotland forged a way for their beasts through inhospitable country, taking them to sell at the trysts in Crieff or Falkirk for onward journeying to England. With 50 or 60 animals to each drover, they avoided 'the highways which distress the feet of the bullocks, and the turnpikes which annoy the spirit of the drover' as described in *The Drove Roads of Scotland* by ARB Haldane. He also evoked them as bears of men smelling of heather and peat smoke who might be knitting stockings as they went. Each night they would stop to graze at wayside stopping points known as 'stances', and often slept in the open, or in inns or cottages when enclosure of land became common.

The practice flourished until a number of factors brought about its rapid demise in the second half of the 19th century. These included the development of cattle shipping, increasing restrictions which forced cavalcades onto made roads and necessitated the animals to be shoed, and rising costs for overnight stances, grazing and tolls.

Newtonmore Riding Centre provided our pack ponies and owner Ruaridh Ormiston, whose family have been in Badenoch for 150 years, accompanied us. His great-grandfather Edward Ormiston was head stalker at Gaick Estate, just a little west of our route through Glen Feshie, and used to walk to Blair Atholl to do his courting and to swap Highland ponies with Atholl Estates for breeding stock. Ruaridh felt he was honouring his family's history by travelling these now little-used hill tracks.

Ruaridh's Highland ponies have bloodlines to two mares bought for the Deer Forest of Gaick from John Cameron or 'Corry' of Corriechollie in Lochaber. The son of an innkeeper, Corry had started out as a barefoot drover's boy but grew a huge droving business of his own. He acquired fortunes in the early nineteenth century, owning as many as thirty farms in Lochaber. He was reputed to have driven cattle and sheep to Falkirk every year for fifty years with droves stretching between five and seven miles long. Ruraidh told us how Corry reputedly rode the 120 miles from Falkirk to Muir of Ord through night and day carrying bread and cheese in his pocket for himself and a bottle of porter for his pony.

We called our journey a 'drove' but with ten pack ponies we barely resembled the real thing. Only wealthier drover-dealers would have had a pony and we had just two cows, a red and a black, Carly and Clare, brought along by Ruaridh for the first day. The red tape of livestock movements since the Foot and Mouth outbreak made it too difficult to take them any further.

Herded with sticks from behind, they lumbered along, peering mischievously through long fringes, apparently relishing the casual gait of migration. Despite their placidity, their wide horns looked distinctly sharp when they swung their heads in our direction. Apparently easier to handle in a herd, they took their chances to turn every now and again and run for home, having us stumbling across the tussocky grass between Tromie Bridge and Glen Feshie shouting and waving sticks. I imagine the drovers to have been more dignified, and such was Ruaridh's rapport with the beasts that he seemed able to drive them with his voice alone.

It allowed me to imagine a time when moving with your animals would have been a common event and an enjoyable one, as suggested by Alexandra Stewart's account of her father walking the 28 miles from Glen Lyon to Glen Almond to fetch a white cow from his cousin in the late nineteenth century. She imagined him relishing his slow walk back with the cow. 'All his life my father seemed to preserve the doting eye that poets share with little children. I don't believe he was ever bored in his own countryside from the early days as a herd boy... For a man like my father, this walk would be alive with the lore and legend of nearly two thousand years, and the activity all about him of his own time.' He arrived home to be reprimanded by his wife for the ugliness of the new cow, who, however, proved to be a good milker.

When you *ride* a pony it's usually clear who's in control. The rider has reins and voice but also the power of her legs and back, the strength of her body. On foot you depend more on head-to-head proximity, and your voice, a hand on the pony's nose, the occasional titbit to induce rapport. This gap between control and trust requires the human-pony relationship to be reciprocal, demanding respect on both sides. It feels more egalitarian than riding.

By necessity we were often strung out in a moving line and couldn't easily converse with each other, so we talked more to the pony: 'Good lad, or fellow, or girl, or lassie. No. Steady. Walk on. Whoah.' There were so many things to say. Walking as a twosome, six legs between you, shoulder to shoulder, heads nodding in time, is in some ways more difficult than riding. It demands concentration and makes you more vulnerable to injury. Most of us had one of our feet ground under a hoof at some point but Vyv outlined how in a simple accident on a narrow path, a pony might catch your heel, causing you to fall forward. The pony's forward momentum would then march its half tonne weight along your spine.

At the beginning of the journey we had been given what seemed slightly contradictory advice. We were told that the ponies needed us to guide them – where best to put their feet, how to keep out of trouble in bogs and on steep ground. They needed to be able to trust us. But we were also told that they would need a very long rein, giving them the freedom to pick their own way, to jump if necessary, swerve out of danger. It suggested that their wayfinding was superior to ours and that they would know the best route. So which was right - did they need us or us them?

Despite many of us being experienced hill-walkers used to wild terrain and camping out, this journey was made serious by having the ponies with us. We knew how to deal with injury to ourselves but if any of the ponies had been hurt, it would have been devastating. Few of us had probably appreciated the implications of this beforehand. Jean said she was moved by this increased sense of responsibility and by the trust the ponies put in us. She described Marigold as her teacher and steady companion, who still looked to her to be guided despite the pony's considerable experience. Marigold's calmness helped both Jean and the younger ponies who were taking such a journey for the first time.

Ailsa, the pony who began the journey nervy and unreliable, was taken in hand by someone experienced who jollied Ailsa through difficult terrain with reassurances and laughter. When I commented on it, she revealed that she didn't always feel relaxed, teetering at the top of a slippery bank, or fording a river, but was projecting confidence to help Ailsa. It worked.

In my teenage riding-stable days I'd never had a single pony of my own to establish a relationship with. The longed-for partnership I read about in *Jill Enjoys Her Ponies* and the *Flambards* books was elusive. I was just one more gawky teenager trying too hard to love Big Brother and Brett and Trampas and to be loved back, but mostly being sullenly ignored as I slid on saddles and bridles and brought them buckets of water and bowls of pony nuts. As busy riding school ponies, they were probably dulled by over-work.

The term 'Highland Ponies' perhaps gives the wrong impression of our pack animals. This is a breed that is both robust and spirited, eager and individual, and they can be as tall as 15'1" hands (just over five foot at the shoulder) and great weight-bearers. Traditionally they've been used for livestock management, droving, bringing deer off the hill, but are mostly now used as riding ponies.

We were supposed to be dedicated to one particular pony over the course of the journey but for various reasons this wasn't always possible. To start with I was often leading Zeno. I'd ridden him on a trip to Newtonmore Riding Centre two years before and remembered him as alert, intelligent and willing to go if asked. But at first I liked him less from the ground. He was restless when we paused and towed me towards the lushest grass. He seemed to have put himself in charge because he was stronger. I felt slightly humiliated. I already trusted his surefooted bravery but was less sure about his personal skills.

One day at lunch I shared my oatcakes with him, and then he

picked up my aluminium thermos flask, raised his head high, and rolled it between his teeth, pinching it flat (his little joke).

'You've been Zeno-ed', said Ruaridh.

Gradually though, our purpose and ways of doing things became shared and we learnt what to expect of each other. Zeno seemed to become more patient. I was kinder to him and led him straight to the best grass when we stopped.

On the second day, we climbed high out of Glen Feshie, into smir. With more ponies than expected and therefore few spare hands, and with only Ruaridh with us from the stables, we wound up through thickening mist onto Meall an Uillt Chreagaich where our comforting, firm track ended. I looked at the map properly now. A double line narrowed to a single one. There followed a steeply contoured gully to cross, taking us to the summit of Leathad an Taobhain at around 3,000 feet and then a pathless traverse across a high plateau to link us to the Minigaig Pass.

We paused on the slope just above the gully. There was no obvious path for the steep descent through peat hags to a small burn. A couple of scouts went ahead to look for the best way across. The ponies were restless. Zeno wheeled around me, barging into others. I was afraid of him being above me on the steep ground, his weight slipping towards me.

Torr, one of two young grey ponies who were brothers, now became edgy. 'He's panicking,' his leader said, as he frisked around her.

Ruaridh was beckoning us on from the perch he'd made on the facing hill. Whilst we'd all managed fine on the slow climb up the track, Vyv now, understandably, didn't seem confident in our ability to cross this ground. She warned us, 'It becomes a thousand times more difficult when you're not on a path'. She'd already told us how quickly a pony can break through peat that walkers would skip over, ending up belly deep and in serious trouble.

There were differences of opinion. There was a lack of clarity over who should take decisions. I was returned to childhood, over-faced and anxious. Not long before this someone had told me of her experience travelling with pack ponies in Chile. When they bolted, the luggage had ended up scattered across a vast area. It was clear that it would only take one pony to break free and the others would follow. The saddle-trees, held on with new leather girths that were still stretching, would inevitably slip and panic the ponies further or perhaps even trip them. I pictured chaos in this bleak place.

I felt sure we were going to have to turn around and that would probably have meant a whole change in plan. Alternative ways south were blocked by hills and the other old passes were too badly eroded for pony travel. Ultimately Vyv led on down into the gully and we followed, lurching, slipping, jumping, but rewarded as we gained dryer ground on the opposite slope by a square of chocolate from Vyv and a sugar-flood of relief. We weren't totally beyond our trial. We still had to navigate our way forward in poor light and mist. But the immediate anxiety of gravity and incline, of being too inexperienced to guide our ponies helpfully, was over. Smiles and chatter returned.

Nothing seemed quite as difficult after that, and as it often does with an adventure in a potentially hostile place, this nervy crossing point came to seem a highlight, a turning point, the peak of our learning and our bonding with each other and the ponies.

From the next summit we processed timelessly across a high plateau with banks of cloud rolling at our side. It felt surreal to be standing by a mist-shrouded trig point with a bunch of ponies, perhaps in one of the remotest places in Britain.

'Here we are,' said Ruaridh when a large lump of white quartz gleamed against the dark heather.

A further glint of white ahead and another more mistily beyond that, confirmed we'd hit the Minigaig Pass. The sense of re-treading this ancient way, the only road shown on Greene's map of 1689 and Moll's map of 1725, was made acute by finding safety after danger as hooves and boots struck into soft peat on our initially gradual descent into Glen Bruar. As the first party to take animals this way for 100 years, we drew confidence from the collective imprint of our forebears, and the line of luminous cairns that led us forward.

'And did those feet!' called out Vyv from the back of the line. I knew exactly what she meant.

Ruaridh had way-marked our route with anecdotes about the prior inhabitants of now-ruined cottages – 'So-and-so lived there and he went off to work in Canada'. The names of crags and corries across this high crossing point which claimed many victims in its time now evoked fairies, a black dog, and even a harpist – Uchd a' Chlarsair. Coire Bhran – raven's corrie – was the summit where drovers would gather before the descent so they could pass through Glen Bruar in formidable numbers and so avoid being accused of trespass.

The final drop of 500 feet from the Minigaig Pass to the head of Glen Bruar would have been a steep 'road', a road that had brought great prosperity to the Glen, once dotted with settlements and sheilings. Its name, Breathless Slope (Uchd na h'Analach) probably reflected the exertion of the climb when travelling north, but we teetered down the narrow, bouldery path, breathless instead with anxiety, into a glen that was all but uninhabited. Golden plover piped us out of the mist and along Glen Bruar, evoking solitude. Ruaridh had remarked on the quietness of the hills since the decline in employment of hill shepherds. An estate of three and a half thousand acres not far away had gone from three full time hill shepherds to one part timer in the last forty years.

It was raining now. We had several flat miles to go on a track. Zeno was restless, tired, clipping the heels of the pony in front. Our line strung out. Bruar Lodge appeared in the distance, a spectre of rest, gradually nearing.

Our difficulties weren't quite over. Without pausing for advice the leaders of two ponies who happened to be in front crossed a bridge over a burn to reach the Lodge. When Ruaridh reached it, he was horrified. Its planks were spaced widely enough for a pony hoof to fall through.

'We could have had broken legs; ponies put down,' he said. 'Always stop and ask if you're not sure.'

The rest of us scrambled down into the burn and up the other side, our charges now agitated and becoming difficult to handle in the rain and disorder.

Three girls welcomed our tetchy arrival with smiles and carrots for the ponies. Before we left the next morning, they asked us all to sign the visitors' book. I imagine those pages years later resurrecting our journey: 'Remember when those "drovers" came through in all that rain?' And so it felt we laid our own story over the ones we revisited along the way, a line teased from a once great web of mountain thoroughfares.

Having successfully carved our way from Newtonmore across that high, remote stretch of the southern Cairngorms and the Grampian hills, on Day Three our party approached Blair Atholl. We descended towards the valley, a campsite, the promise of a hot shower and a day's rest, emerging out of 'wilderness' into a place I associated with home in Aberfeldy just the other side of the A9.

We were calm now and the ponies echoed it back to us. Our human steps rhymed with theirs. It was as if we now saw the landscape and our way through it with their sensibilities and had 'got' their rhythms, walking at a pace which maintained our line so that no-one was stressed by being left behind; so that we operated as a 'herd' in a chain of understanding. These were some of the journey's happiest moments; a procession of ten sets of clopping hooves, pacing boots, grey and brown Highland pony backsides rolling in step ahead. Sometimes it seemed that the line we drew through the land re-animated the original path; visually highlighting its curves and kinks and restoring it to life with elemental sounds – heartbeat, hoof beat, voice. It was a contented motion interrupted only by the need to stop and adjust a slipping saddle or to wait for someone.

As we paraded down the avenue that passes the front steps of the white Gothic-spired Blair Castle I felt intensely aware of the fluid movement of our line; the beat of our feet and clatter of forty hooves on tarmac. Zeno pricked his ears, a warm bulk next to me who I rewarded now with pats and murmurs. We must have made a bedraggled, raggle-taggle spectacle, having come through heavy rain with our loaded panniers and muddy boots. Neatly dressed visitors to the castle watched us go past. I heard a woman answer her daughter's question with: 'They're travelling with their ponies, love'. I felt a great rush of pride; tears almost. I was a person of the road with my pony beside me, a pony that had become so much more than a luggage-carrier.

Later, we led the ponies from our campsite to the gate into their field. Free from tack and panniers, there was something sweet in this end-of-day ritual as we released them from head-collars to roll away their sweat-stains and play spirited games up and down a grassy slope. Our camp meal was accompanied by thundering hooves and squeals from the next field to which we answered 'yeehaaa!' way into the long midsummer night.

The rhythms of any camping journey – pitching tents, cooking, sleeping – were extended by looking after the ponies' needs – untacking, turning them out, finding water. The compassion we needed to find for our animals even when we were tired and hungry, characterised the culture of our expedition, and softened it.

Sleeping so close to them, separated only by a fence, seemed to increase our intimacy. In the mornings we'd crawl from our tents to find the ponies lying down or sitting with noses dropped and closed eyes. They gradually got up and gathered near the fence, waiting to see what would happen next. Just as we commented on them – 'Look at Marigold rolling; she's over once, twice,' or, 'they've become good pals,' – we imagined them in turn commenting on us. 'Look, those two have their tents next to each other again,' and, 'they never stop eating, do they?' We enjoyed their apparent wish to be near us as we sat on the grass chatting, cooking evening meals or breakfast. Perhaps they even commented on the diversity of our porridge rituals. Methods of cooking and serving varied from instant oats out of a sachet with jam added; a variety cooked with whole milk and jumbo oats served with almonds and figs; and another with Greek yoghurt and strawberries.

Over the week the animals became like members of our extended family with distinct personalities and allegiances. Sarah reflected afterwards on what it had meant to her: 'You're sharing a really hard journey with an animal that you seem to be making a connection with. You're concentrating so much on keeping the pony happy and safe and well fed, it takes the harshness of the journey away.' She found something almost mystical in the silent communication, the rhythm established through so much time spent together, the way the ponies seem to know when the end of the journey was coming.

With their heads nodding, breathing softly next to us, they had clip-clopped their way into our hearts. And their names rang in our mouths like a poem: Torr, Zeno, Bean, Blue, Breagh, Alice, Ailsa, Micky, Mack, and Marigold. In the days after we left them and went home, they made frequent appearances in my dreams.

The journey also gathered people to us. Despite our often remote location, and the sense at times of a haunted, abandoned landscape, each night we had extra company of some sort; folk joining us with songs or stories, or hosting us in their fields and steadings. At Newtonmore and Blair Atholl, 'Meet the Drovers' events gathered local people and tourists to pat the ponies and ask about the way. When we were on roads Ruaridh chatted with drivers at open car windows. The Highland pony fraternity turned out to meet him and his famous Jack Russell, Rosie, and to chew over old stories and bring news between estates divided by ranges of hills and time.

We had no doubt that these gatherings were an important part of being on the road. As Joyce reminded us, it's the accumulation of small ceilidhs that will change the world – creative people talking and making things happen out of shared experience.

After Blair Atholl, a change in logistics and people on the journey meant that some ponies were ridden rather than led. This changed the feel of our procession but was a relief for those with the sorest feet. Two days after leaving Blair Atholl, with local families following us in a carnivalesque wake, we travelled the sunny miles down Glen Fearnach, and then, accompanied by the fanfare of the River Ardle, on the Cateran Trail into Kirkmichael. Our final event there was on the site of a once-important cattle market at the convergence of several drove roads.

It was clear by now that a nerve had been tingled by our quirky procession; a way of life suggested because we were moving alongside animals. Perhaps it raised a folk memory, barely lost, of our partnership with working animals and with the land. Vyv often said of her many experiences of travelling with ponies, as opposed to walking or cycling, that they bring you into tune with the landscape around you, make you feel more part of it and allow wildlife to come closer; allow you to notice more.

Our journey had seemed so much longer and made us feel so much smaller than its 60 miles implied. The footprints and hoofprints we left behind were ephemeral, but the experience would remain deeply etched in our memories. Despite our mobile phones, Gore-Tex jackets and town lives, we had added to the beat of age-old, repeated footfall on the road and got hoof beats echoing through the glens once more.

The Dogs' Route

Spean Bridge
Loch Treig
Blackwater reservoir
Kingshouse
Stars!
Gorton Bothy
WHW
Swim
Inverolnan (pub)
Rannoch moor
Cailliche

Glen Lyon P.O.
last shop

Invervar
(last bed)

River Lyon

River Tay

home

Loch Lyon

Charlotte's
house

Loch
Tay

← Direction of travel
(1st)

A drove road between Perthshire and the Isle of Skye, Scotland

In the course of a walk, we usually find out something about our companion, and that is true even when we travel alone.
In Praise of Walking, Thomas A Clark

I approached the slipway of the Glenelg-to-Kylerhea ferry on the early evening of the thirteenth day, hastened by an imminent Force Eight gale that might stop the ferry running. High winds were already whipping up a frenzy of waves and rocking caravans on a south-facing beach campsite. A turned-out tent showed me its pale yellow guts. I put on more clothes and quickened my step.

The main purpose of my journey was to reach the Isle of Skye and I had almost done it. I looked back at the village of Glenelg, strung-out and crouching below the hills. A little along the bay, Gleann Beag sliced inland, towered over by Beinn a' Chapuill and the serrated skyline of this northwest mainland. In the preceding days' appalling weather, my route had threaded between these steep walls and through a half-shut eye of memory.

When I reached the rise above the slipway, I saw the ferry chortling crab-wise towards Kylerhea with a single car on board. It was fighting the formidable current just as the cattle that were once swum across in the opposite direction must have done. A car pulled up and a couple got out looking hopeful. I felt reassured. If there were accomplices in my escape from the mainland, surely the ferry would have to run?

I was walking a 200 mile journey from my front door in Perthshire across the mountainous wild land of northwest Scotland where I've spent so much time over the last twenty-five years. My route had been trodden before me by the numerous cattle-drovers who once herded animals south to market at this time of year, streaming in black ghost-lines in the opposite direction. Along with the outer isles, Skye became one of the most important suppliers of cattle known as 'kyloes', a small black breed considered superior. The practice of droving these cattle to market started in the early sixteenth century. Gathering them at Sligachan and Broadford on Skye, and travelling ten to twelve miles each day, they drove them 200 miles south to the Tryst at Crieff or Falkirk.

After the sales, whilst the men stayed drinking in the Inns, or went further south and returned to Scotland later by boat, their dogs went home ahead of them, stopping to rest at the same inns or 'stances' as on their journey down. I was travelling in the opposite direction to the drovers, which made this sea crossing near the end of my journey as opposed to their beginning. I felt that I was taking the dogs' route.

Cattle from all over Skye and the Outer Isles would have been drawn into a single point at Kylerhea, as many as 8,000 a year. Haldane remarks of this sea crossing: 'To one watching from the hill overlooking the Kyle how the tide sweeps like a great river northward to the junction of Loch Duich and Lochalsh, or how when the current sets south, tide and wind meet in Glenelg Bay in a welter of white and angry water, it may seem that this crossing of the Kyle marks, as little else could do, the hardihood, the courage and skill of the drovers of Scotland.'

Linked by means of a rope noose put under the jaw of each cow and tied to the tail of the one in front, a string of six to eight cows would be formed. With a man at the stern of the boat holding the lead cow, the boatmen would take across 300 to 400 cattle in a few hours, seeking the eddy at either side and resisting capsize. This was perhaps the crux of the journey, the part that might inspire fear, and where the drovers could lose their investment. It demanded of them a hero's response.

Like a series of thresholds, there had been many crossings on my journey so far - rivers, railways, roads, the Great Glen fault-line, mountain passes, transitions between rock types, the boundaries of mental geography. Each threshold arose to demand from me a commitment of sorts, to the next step in a new terrain. This one before me, across water, had now had taken on a mythic weight. I was in no danger of life or loss, but there was anxiety, the need gnawing at me to put the territory of the past behind and complete a journey.

'We'll get you across, don't worry,' the ferryman said to me. 'But we might not get you back.'

Three men hauled on ropes, clanked ramps and chains, and then The Glenachulish was underway. She's the last of the manually operated turntable ferries once common in the Highlands and Islands, kept running by local people who leased the vessel in 2006, the previous year, and then raised the necessary funds to buy her.

The men swivelled the turntable, so that we revolved away from Glenelg's shore to look ahead at Skye. Anxiety segued into excitement as I stood storm-whipped on the open deck with the couple from the car and the ferrymen, and we talked of swimming cows and the likelihood of the force eight materialising. I looked ahead at the cluster of painted cottages on the other side and the road zigzagging high over the Kyelrhea pass.

We met the island with a bang and clash. The car doors opened, slammed shut. I walked up the metal ramp and onto the road. I'd planned to walk another two or three days from here; to reach Sligachan before considering my journey complete. The main thing was that I was across. I had reached the Isle of Skye. I decided to get as far as Broadford and then decide whether to call it a day. When the couple offered me a lift, I took it.

It was half my lifetime ago, perhaps in 1983, that I first went to Skye on my second visit to Scotland. I went with a friend, Jonti, who my ex-partner Neil and I were visiting in the English Lakes where he worked as an instructor for Outward Bound. It was an impulse trip for the three of us, and displaced so suddenly from the Lakes, I spent the first couple of days mourning the small tucked-in valleys, woodlands and cosy pubs. I felt exposed against Skye's harsh lines, the huge scale of everything, the exchange of the lyrical for opera. It was as if I'd arrived there too quickly.

It was one of those famous late-Mays when high pressure creaked open blue skies over the west of Scotland day after day. We camped at Glenbrittle with guy ropes overlapping those of other climbers, and queued for toilets every morning. We had Jonti's collie, Spot, with us and he and I were thrown together for company and un-ambitious walks on beaches and by waterfalls while Neil and Jonti did the overnight traverse of the Black Cuillin's prickly and precarious ridge in perfect conditions.

Whilst its grandeur can still shock and shiver me, that trip was the beginning of a long relationship with Skye – cycling, walking, climbing, and more recently working as a writer in its schools.

Jonti went to work in Colorado and never returned to live in Britain. Still a man of the mountains, I owe him much for introducing me to the possibilities of the hills. Back then, he also made shoes. They had flat white crepe soles and round toes. Made with brightly coloured leather, they were boldly stitched with raised seams, just like Cornish pasties. So we called them 'pasty shoes'.

He made a pair of baby's boots, cut roughly from red and yellow leather. They were lined with sheepskin and held with large uncompromising stitches onto a thick crepe sole. They were both sweet and rugged. I somehow ended up with them, whether as a gift or left behind for safekeeping, I can't now remember.

The boots have moved with me from house to house for over 20 years, gradually accumulating significance. Eventually they took up residence in the rarely-opened drawer in which darken the letters, diaries, wedding and funeral mementoes that I'm somehow both afraid of, and want to cherish. I suppose they were waiting patiently for the time when I would have a child of my own to wear them.

Those first days in September when I set out from Perthshire were the year's summer. Squadrons of dragonflies hummed around my head, scabious and meadowsweet brushed my bare calves, and the air was still, sweetened with birdsong. My familiar places close to home sprang up – bright cold pools I sometimes swim in, birch tunnels I cycle through, local ways up Carn Gorm or Ben Lawers. When I break a cycle ride or an autumn walk at the Post Office at Bridge of Balgie, delicate cups are delivered upon flowered saucers and filled and refilled with tea.

This start in a familiar landscape joined up my day walks, gave me the pleasure of naming places, but also noticing the shifts in colour, and the slow changes in the bulky shape of Ben Lawers as I skirted its sides. It was strange but lovely that for the first two nights I was near enough home to stay with local friends.

After three golden days in Glen Lyon, the wind rose, cloud lowered and I had my first night camping, with the river rumbling past my tent just downstream from Pubil dam. I walked the first half of that day with friends Sue and Iain who met me at the dam. We walked west past Loch Lyon, dammed up and bleak without trees, untouched by tarmac, and leading up into a confluence of high glens. The turrets of the fortress that arcs northeast from Beinn Dorain in the south to Beinn a Creachain, had walled me out of the 'beyond' by this route until now. Then the others had to turn back and we said our goodbyes.

The slight rise of Glen Meran took me northwards, hair dampening as I climbed into mist, feet following where the deer had trodden paths. The weight of my rucksack gnawed an ache deep into my hip joints. In the late afternoon, Glen Meran spilt me onto Rannoch

Moor. My eyes sought features on the blank bog: pylons stalking along the Fort William railway line; an occasional Scots Pine isolating itself as a dark silhouette, flattened by dull light. I followed a quad bike trail to find the 'creep', a low gap under the embanked railway. My feet were pulled at by gloopy peat bog. In crazed fluorescence, green and red mosses caught at my eye as if displaced from a world of coral reefs. I abandoned the preserve of dry boots and socks. For the first time on the walk I was out of my comfort zone, wet and peat-splattered, travelling very slowly in an unknown land.

Alone, the meshing of rhythm, thought and observation had me inventing songs and rhymes. Lyrics were delivered in my head to the tune of *Walking on the Moon* by The Police.

'I hope your legs don't break
Walking Rannoch Moor.
A boat's what you should take
Walking Rannoch Moor.'

And so on. Another long-distance solo walker I've come across imagined he was a bearer of news between families of cows separated by distance. When they rushed over to the fence to meet him it was as if he was a mail-ship arriving. He passed on news of Sister Agnes's sore nipples and so on. The mind plays games when left to talk to itself, and for my part I enjoy this slightly off-beat creativity.

I spent that night in a bothy I came across by chance by the Water of Tulla. In the morning, sun blasted the valley into a tumble of white rock and blue river and outlined the beckoning hills of the west. I took everything outside to dry on the grass and stood by my front door. The rattle of the train to Fort William approached, growing into a gallop opposite me, and then steadying on its looping journey north. I imagined how I must look from the train, a wifie outside her cottage, miles from anywhere.

I descended towards Loch Tulla, breathing in heather scent as the hills cleared of cloud ahead of me. I hailed the hooked peak of Stob Ghabhar that I'd climbed on a day of hard snow and sun a couple of winters before. Only half an hour later I reached something else familiar at my left shoulder; a climb with friends up Ben Achaladair about 15 years before. I remembered how in the first few morning miles we had dallied through the Black Wood of Crannach which sits grandly under Beinn a' Creachain. Later, caught out by early snow and the change from British Summer Time, we'd ended up benighted and slithering through wet snow and peat bog, pulled by two dogs on leads towards lights in the valley. Today I looked at the wood from the other side of the river, sunlight highlighting the shelves of Scots Pine foliage.

The line of the walk was taking me out of familiarity and then returning me to it. Crossing thresholds and linking places. I took notice when I read in Thomas A Clark's poem *In Praise of Walking*: 'We can walk between two places and in so doing establish a link between them, bring them into a warmth of contact, like introducing two friends.' I'd come to walk the drovers' route, but perhaps it had partly appealed to me because of this linking of memories.

A heron at the edge of the water caught my eye. Then an electronic bleep stopped me; I had walked back into mobile phone territory. The phone had hung on to a message sent sometime between days two and five, between Glen Lyon and Glen Tulla. It was from my Edinburgh friend Kathy Jarvis who I've walked and climbed many Scottish hills with. She's passionate about the high Andes and runs a trekking business there, but I knew she'd be setting out on a brand new adventure during my time away.

Her message read: 'Lewis Jarvis born ten am today! All well! x'

I whispered a Hurrah for Kathy and for Lewis, mentally threading another bright jewel on my string of journey-beads. This one though seemed misted with a little sadness. The heron slowly mobilised its elbowing wings, took off and soared upstream.

Deer helped me on this walk, where the way was soft and the paths laid by streaming cattle had been lost. Their subtle communal tracks led to crossing points on burns and found the harder ground on the sides of valleys. The animals sometimes showed themselves in a leap across my path, a roar filtered through mist on a hillside, a head turning over a shoulder before it galloped away. But mostly they were invisible guides, laying prints in instinctive lines through the land.

At the other extreme, Thomas Telford laid a cobbled trail between the famous droving inns at Inveroran and Kingshouse. It had me swinging rhythmic strides for ten short miles as if the scale of the map had changed. A marching tune, a Gay Gordons rang in my head. Legs and feet, breath and heart beat in a harmony that seemed to echo the pulse of the Earth, perfectly synchronised with slow shifts of scene. It energised my body and my mind, settled me in to the pace of thought and conversation. This section of my route coincided with the West Highland Way and the steady surface was accompanied by talk and by the metronomic clickety-clack of walking poles hitting rock.

I fell into step with two lads I'd met in the pub the night before. Then I left them with a group of cheery Germans who stopped on the summit of the first hill to brew up coffee away from the midges (or so they thought in that first, misleading sixty-second curfew). I passed on to walk with two women from London, and then from them to two young Israeli men struggling under 25 kilo packs, and demanding reassurance about three words that were shivering them with apprehension about what was ahead: 'The Devil's Staircase'.

Unlike a cocktail party, no excuse was ever needed to pass on to the next conversation. It happened naturally with the tying of a bootlace. Over a long lunch in the Kingshouse bar the same people reconvened. Boots were removed, blisters compared and patched up. With anxious glances through the window, plans were moulded, tested on others, coalitions formed on missions to escape midges, rain, being alone, or the desolate camping ground outside the bar which had me inclined to agree with Dorothy Wordsworth when she said she'd never seen, 'such a miserable, such a wretched place'.

I don't think I've ever struck up conversation with anyone in a motorway services, and yet the pubs and cafes on my route were rich with encounter. It was as if my solitude inclined me to drop barriers and delight in sharing experience. With walkers there's always subject-matter – the route, weather, memories of past walks, advice on new places. Such journey-talk is a small step from how we choose to live our lives and what we value. It's not, to me, superficial.

I clung for a while to the sense of a moving carnival, the nod to a previous time when drovers would have been funnelled from the north and met at this Inn for noisy conviviality. But in the end I chose solitude, pressed on over a pathless *bealach* to spend the next two nights isolated from roads or company until Spean Bridge.

Dialogue pattered on in my head, in my journal, between my feet and the land, and between my back and the ground as I slept. It was company that felt as real as the jollity of that morning. The mind that goes on a long walk invents and makes jokes with itself, raises memories to the surface, and sorts problems. To me, not walking and not ever being alone would be to deny a part of myself.

Halfway through my journey I crossed the Great Glen, a wide, ruler-straight trench that splits the Highlands in two, linking North Sea and Atlantic. A rift valley that is marked by deep lochs, it was formed volcanically over 400 million years ago, and then deepened by glacial activity. It's still said to be slightly unstable.

This rift also delineates the half of Scotland I chose, and the other half that my ex-partner, Neil, chose. The lochs deepened and schisms grated further apart once we were entrenched on either side. We hadn't lost touch since the final division seven years before, but we'd avoided each others' immediate territory, and that avoidance of an area where I'd once spent a lot of time, left something not quite resolved for me in my emotional geography. This time, on foot, on a route that led directly between my door and his, it began to seem a subconscious plot, as if the walk was a line of stitching to repair a rip.

I took with me six pink-jacketed OS Landranger maps, posting them back to myself as I walked off them to the north and west. The most frayed and tattered were my local map, number 51, *Loch Tay and Surrounding Area*, and 33 – *Loch Alsh, Glen Shiel and surrounding area*. Open them randomly and the contrast is striking. The latter is densely packed with contours, scuffling crag marks and writhing fingers of loch. Close, undisciplined lines saturate the map with colour. The Loch Tay map, swirled by widely-spaced contour lines and swaying lochs, has a much paler effect on paper.

It was this difference that took Neil west onto that side of the fault-line, onto Map 33, where the peaks are corrugated, the pubs loud with joke and tale and music, and off-beam lives are nurtured and accepted.

Having discarded three maps at Spean Bridge Post Office on day nine, I crossed over the Caledonian Canal and the Great Glen at Gairlochy. The hills of the east behind me were muscular, like the rounded limbs of horses, sheep, humans. The hills ahead were gnarled, angular, revealing as much rock as turf and spined like reptiles. They were split by steep valleys. I was swamped by a sense of insecurity. I felt I needed to be stronger, more alert. My anxiety was sharpened by a forecast for two days of 'incessant' and 'tumultuous' rain and gales.

The soles of my boots had become so worn that I worried about their grip on steep rock and bog that I knew was before me, teeming after several days of rain with multiplying burns. I had rivers to cross, I had a pass to go over, and then I had to walk through a high-sided glen to where it pinched and narrowed. After my experience in Norway, I was far less sure of my feet; knowing what could happen with a simple slip or trip.

On the twelfth day I woke up in a high valley above Kinloch Hourn. My hands were numb as I took the tent down. I looked up at the hills around me, knobbly and devious, the tops now smudged with first snow. The pylons that had been at my shoulder all along Loch Quoich, were now forced into an off-kilter dance. One stood low on a small terrace here, the next up there on the top of a steep crag, straining the wires towards vertical. The next found footing on a low platform of rock. They played hopscotch, impishly finding stepping stones across the landscape.

Blood pumped back into my hands as I started to walk, and a whisper of confidence crept back. My journey began to reassert itself. I followed the pylon line steeply up the fjord-like side of Loch Hourn behind the big house. It took me through a rock clefted as if by the stroke of a giant's axe. Just the other side of its summit, I stopped and the mist blanket allowed glimpses, and then obscured again, the big hills that storm upwards here – the Saddle and its various outliers, including Sgurr na Sgine. I laid my rucksack briefly onto a nearby rock. It took me a few moments to notice that three horizontal slabs had been aligned with three vertical ones. This 'bench' rang with three absences. Weary drovers leant on sticks, regaining their breath after the hard slog up, and before a steep descent. The dogs snuffed about nearby, the cattle roaming for grass. For a second it eased the loneliness of the route I saw ahead.

The ancient users of this through-way would be absent and silent today, but as I started the descent, and then the next climb, their road began to reassure me. I felt its ancient quality under my feet. It contoured the hills thoughtfully, found rock, eased me through the rough terrain. It wound up and down through the hills, offering glimpses of Loch Hourn to the west, and to the curmudgeonly skyline of Druim Fada. Ahead, the pylons stalked into the high mist, and the nipple point of Beinn nan Caorach was there and then gone, there and then gone, a beacon marking the west side of the pass at Bealach Aoidhdailean.

The river I walked down to was gurgling with fast-moving laughter. It gave no hint of where the cattle would have crossed, except perhaps for the wide shingly area, when shallower. I was forced back upstream. With trousers rolled to the knee, I released my feet from the soggy warmth of wool and leather and they fought for blood and feeling against the current and slippery rock. That was the first of three such crossings that day, which slowed and wearied me as thick rain set in and I climbed through the mist to the *bealach* at 1500 feet. In the final

Broadford
Kylerhea
Glenelg
Neil's
Pylon Glen
Stars
Loch Hourn
Kinloch Hourn

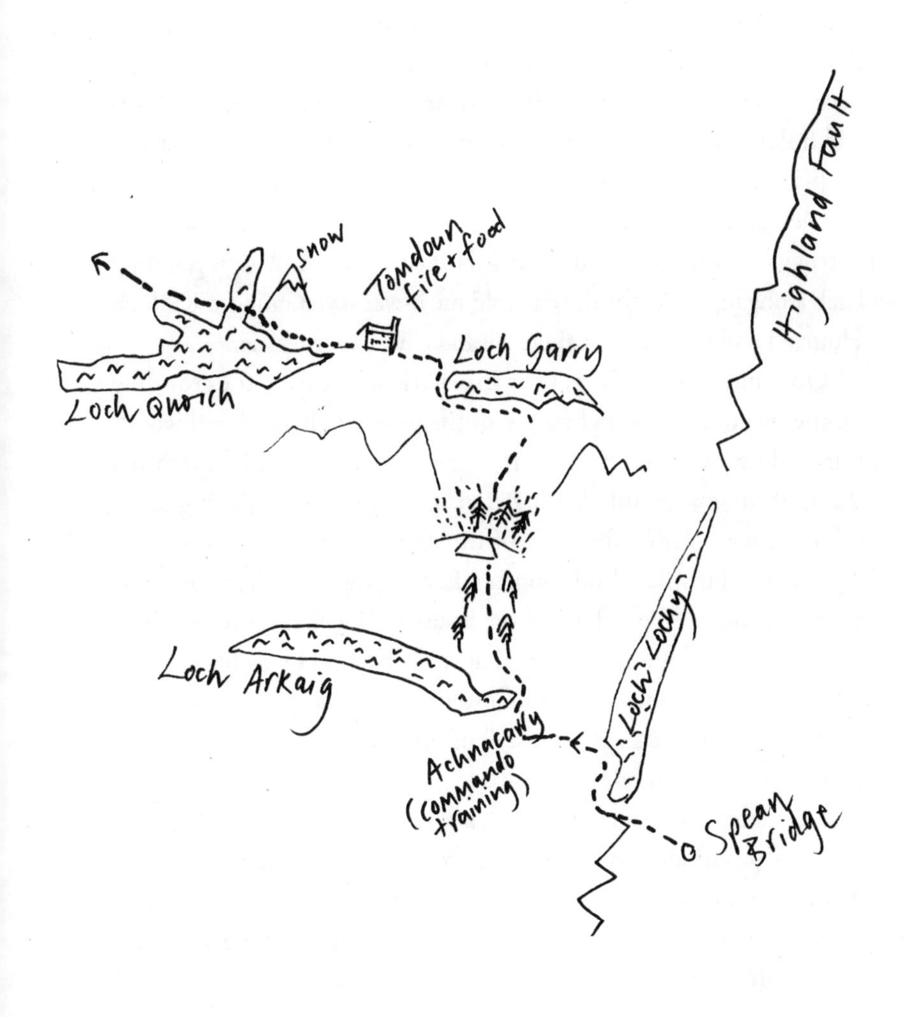

← Direction of travel (2nd)

sharp ascent the wires of the pylons sang to me like distant engines.

I looked ahead down Glen Aoidhdailean which I knew as a kind of old, back gateway into Gleann Beag. It must have been at least eight years since I'd come this way, perhaps more. A bleak sweep of river, pylons and path were cradled in a glen that pushes down for two miles to a small square of plantation. From there, I recalled, the path twists around a grassy stretch of meadow at Suardal to cross the river that flows down Gleann Beag. A hard steady track then follows the river, becomes tarmac a few miles downstream, eventually meeting the sea and linking Gleann Beag to the village of Glenelg around the coast.

Just before the final river crossing at Suardal, I reached a high wooden gate. It was sodden and heavy, wedged on a high rock, and I struggled to lift it. The despair I felt tasted of salt. A sign pointing back along my route for the day told me it was seven miles to Kinloch Hourn. I had set out from there six and a half hours earlier.

Once into Gleann Beag, I felt an electric startle from the crowding in, the breath-stealing tightening of the glen. Birch and hazel woods tumbled down beside steep white burns on either side. I'd forgotten the high drama of this land. Beinn a' Chapuill's steepening spine followed me on the other side of the river, calling my memory. On my fortieth birthday, Midsummer's Eve, a gang of us had spent the evening eating and drinking in the house in the glen-bottom. When we went out at three am, we saw that sunlight was kissing pink the tip of the craggy summit and we followed it as if chasing a rainbow, lay down at the top and slept as crystals of frost melted on the moss under us and the sun warmed from above.

I threaded on through the glen, aware that up high on that hill to my right, just hidden above the hazel wood, breathing air and sunlight, was the house Neil had built. I found him and his partner, Amy, in the Glen which they've helped revive from a time not long ago when human life here comprised a mouse-infested crofter's cottage and 500 acres of sheep-impoverished land.

Salad, fruit and vegetable crops now thrive in poly-tunnels and are sold to local homes and businesses in the summer. There's a sustainable energy business, small sheds where visiting friends can stay, and a horse-drawn wagon with an espresso machine serving take-aways to visitors to the historic brochs. Lives are lived here, people congregate and have parties to celebrate the place.

I found remnants of myself too. The foot-long whips of young trees I'd helped plant along the sides of the hill track now towered leafy and flamboyant over head height, delighted with the soil. Buckets of wet cement I'd helped carry for foundations had solidified and grown a house. But the opportunity I'd had to be part of this place, to participate in its fruitfulness, was long past. I'd chosen another way.

Despite the kindnesses, the tea and food and drying off, the exchanges of news about mutual friends from university days, I suddenly felt the need for movement. Pressed in this tight drama of valley, water, rock, memory, I needed to breathe, to be alone again, to work out what to do next. I needed to reclaim the journey; to prove that the line I'd partly invented behind me could also continue forwards.

I walked the remaining tight-throated two miles of the glen before it opened to sheep-cropped grass and shingle beach at Eilanreach. Turning the corner, a view spread north across the water to Kylerhea with its shore-side cottages under the hills. I walked along the shingle, as sun broke from behind boulders of cloud and glinted for an hour. The big sky let me breathe. There was seaweed smell and gulls' tumble. Waves frothed by the wind were beating onto the shore. I walked towards the crossing point, the ferry to Skye. I walked fast.

After crossing to Skye, I found myself tight-rope walking on the cusp of the Autumn Equinox. I found shelter from the rising force eight in a Broadford B+B and thought about what to do.

For the previous thirteen days, the promise of Camasunary had gleamed at the end of my journey in a sweep of bay under the Cuillins on the south of the island. A place of close-cropped grass, a hollow between two ridges, a beach, a haven. I'd imagined myself relaxing there in sunshine, watching birds and reading.

But to include Camasunary meant another day's walking, and with the prospect of further raging weather, I was ready to call it a day. I could honourably consider my journey complete, after all it had been my main intention to reach Skye.

The next morning Philip Tordoff, my host, stood outside the door with me, continuing our conversation about the value of walking the old ways, about what it means to find enlightenment in land and books. Trained as a church minister, he had a soft way of laying words, and I felt my path strangely blessed by him as he offered advice on places on my route. I walked off into a dry morning, gusted past the Co-op, and my boots strode me back into a rhythm. Rather than turning for home, I turned south-west towards Elgol, and the road rose to meet me.

'In particular,' he had said, 'be sure to take a small detour. Climb the hill next to where a red van is parked.'

This chance meeting was how I came to visit High Pastures, one of the several treasures in the casket of that particular day. And Philip Tordoff joined the ranks of my esteemed guides. Foremost amongst them were the drovers – intelligent, hardy businessmen who fashioned the route with understanding of human and animal movement, weather, watercourses and sources of hospitality. They found firm ground and food for the cattle. Their confidence in the best ways through the land later led to stones paved over their line, and later still, in some places such as here, tarmac.

Strath Suardal cradles the Broadford River, and there the lumpen mass of Beinn na Caillich watched me as I walked the windswept valley towards the red van. The hill altered little in shape as I passed south. Eroded and rounded out of red granite unlike the gabbro-corrugated Black Cuillin that I was heading for later that day, it framed itself within the doorway of Cill Chriosd, the ivy-tangled roofless church that sits on an ancient mound.

The cailliche – the old woman or hag goddess – played a central role in a story I'd written three years earlier. Loosely set on one of my local hills, Schiehallion, she was losing her power as Beltane marked the arrival of Spring. She was a goddess of Winter with knuckly cold fingers and a blue face, spreading ice, shattering rocks and clutching at human hearts. In my version, she was attended by creaking herons. The honk of geese heralding her arrival at Samhain and departure at Beltane would be more traditional. In my story, and I suppose in my mind, she was to be feared, a mere hoarse whisper away from death.

The cailliche had been showing herself to me over the summer, cropping up in placenames and folkloric stories, her face outlined on the southern headland at the entrance to Loch Broom and in the names of mountains such as this in Strath Suardal.

I'm not an old woman, and yet if you're considered old once your fertile years are past, I'm heading towards that different way of being. This journey was challenging my body, calling for stamina, energy, strength, mobility. These were qualities of youth. Just before setting off I'd received a letter from my surgery, telling me a test result suggested 'joint disease'. I knew the meaning of the two words individually, but together they meant little. As I held the letter, a picture lurched into my mind of an old man I'd seen inching along a pavement, so bent over that he couldn't look ahead. His wife was leading him, being his eyes. I remembered that I'd bounded past them. I put the letter under a pile of other papers to consider on my return .

Not much beyond the churchyard, near where the road turns west and northwest towards Torrin, I left my rucksack and followed the markers uphill from the red van. On the hill or 'high pastures', deep underneath the summer sheiling dwellings of a more recent people, a system of caves has concealed ritual mysteries of female fertility. Poised between limestone and granite, where water dives and vanishes into the earth, archaeologists are discovering in layers of ash the story of a fire kept burning for 800 years. Where daylight hit the womb-shaped cave floor, objects associated with the Celtic goddess Brigid had been buried.

In this underworld, buried treasure tells of transitions. At the cave entrance – the interface of light and dark – there are quern-stones that made flour from grain; iron-smelting equipment that changed rock to metal. Bones glimmer, highlighting the point between life and death. Around 80 AD the site was ritually filled in, and the cave entrance topped with the skeleton of a young woman, the remains of a five-month old foetus and a two week old child.

People were kneeling in trenches, scraping carefully at layers of history, straining soil through water to look for clues. The scent of discovery was palpable. A woman told me she'd come all the way from South Africa to volunteer for six weeks on the dig. There were a few of us visiting the site, hanging on the words of the archaeologists. We stood out of the wind in a wooden hut, asking questions: 'Could it be... ?' 'What if... ?' We added our speculations to theirs and then grew quiet.

We were balancing at a season of equal dark and light, in a place where the world above meets the world below, and teetering on a geological boundary.

Outside the shed, a white stone stood on the grass. Perhaps two and a half feet high, it had a wide base and a narrowing upright body, shaped into curves and edges like a seated figure. Moulded by water and then buried below, it seemed to have as much in common with a sculpture by Henry Moore or Barbara Hepworth as with Bronze Age remains.

The stone left me with questions. But it also led me back to another place, to which Sue and Iain had taken me on one of the first days of this walk.

We'd climbed into Glen Cailliche above the northwest finger of Loch Lyon. It was a small deviation from the route that would later take me through Glen Meran and onto Rannoch Moor.

Near the burn, amongst green pastures, we found the small house, 'Tigh nam Bodach'. Perhaps two feet high including its turf roof, it has stone walls and a paved floor. Because we were there during the six months of light, the stones of the front wall had been lifted clear to open the house, and seven odd stone figures stood in two lines in front of it.

Licked into curious shapes by burn water, the figures appeared to represent a family. The woman dominates the group. She has a wide, squareish base narrowing into a thin neck, and a spherical head of pink stone. The rest of her brood are smaller and less solid except for one wide squat one, and are also fashioned by the differential wear of water to give their upper edges rims or lines. They have the dignity of figures on Easter Island.

We sat just downhill of them and stared. With low cloud obscuring the high ridge, the sides of the Cailliche valley met perfectly at the roof of the little house. In a windswept but fertile-green place, the house is said by some to be a 'sheiling shrine'. The first thing that would be done as the party arrived each summer to graze the cattle, make cheese, tell stories, was to open up the house and bring out the figures. But even now, the ritual opening and closing of the house is continued at the two ends of the year.

We pondered what force it was that would bring a modern-day ghillie up on his quad bike to officiate and what it meant that something which spoke of fertility was positioned by the burn and glen named for an old woman. Is it that the three phases of womanhood – girlhood, fertility and age – are gathered in one place?

We lingered there in earthy reverence just below the cloud base, putting our hands on the rough, lichen-grained stones as if we they would give us answers. When we walked away through the long grass to the track above the loch, we stopped often to look over our shoulders at the small, powerful presence.

The image of the bold stone woman had stayed with me. She'd given me my 'send off' as I crossed my first real threshold into the unsettled west out of my home territory when Iain and Sue turned for home.

Now, here at High Pastures where orange tape marked the edges of the excavation and enthusiasts scrabbled at discovery with earth-grained hands, she seemed to show herself again, just as I neared the end of my two-week-long journey.

Before I left I asked the archaeologist for his name.

'Martin Wildgoose,' he said.

'Of course,' I thought, hearing an echo of the skein-cries of migration that I'd heard creaking above me over the last days, marking the change in the year. I cast a wry nod at Beinn na Caillich. The hag-goddess was prowling nearby, waiting to be heralded in again by her geese.

I walked back down the grassy slope towards my rucksack, the road, the way ahead. A small figure in a red cagoule moved very slowly ahead of me. It took the road in the same direction, the hood up, arms splaying a bit awkwardly at its sides. It seemed to list like an overloaded boat lashed at by the wind. I caught up quickly and when the figure turned at my greeting, I saw it was the elderly woman who had been in the hut when I arrived at the dig, asking a great many questions. We exchanged a few words of marvel at what we'd witnessed up there and then she told me to go on, otherwise she would hold me up, and it was raining.

I went on, eager to make some headway on the ten miles of road I had to march before the up-and-over on the track to Camasunary. I was also eager to get to the café. I wondered how far the old lady was going.

The village of Torrin hugs a low slope on the eastern side of Loch Slapin. I descended through it, enjoying its bright green meadows and effervescent sprays of orange monbrietia startling against the white cottages. On the other side of the loch the fierce fortress of Bla Bheinn thrust up its craggy skyline, black and gothic.

I sat out several heavy showers in the Blue Shed Café, drank coffee, had soup and toasties. An old BMW motorbike was parked outside, its unconventionally towering luggage flapping string and black plastic. Inside, a tall man with a posh English voice, long wavy brown hair and a weather-beaten face was holding court with a couple on another table. He talked about his motorbike journey, sub-prime mortgages, the world economy, his life story. I wrote in my journal, looked out as sheets of rain obscured and then shimmered on Bla Bheinn's gully-scarred rocks. In the middle of the day a warm fug of travellers' conviviality steamed the windows of the café. Each new arrival had to be helped with the damp-stuck door.

After about 45 minutes the woman in the red cagoule arrived and we were soon sharing a table, she encouraging me to eat some cake. She wore a blue jumper which matched her eyes, and she never stopped smiling. There was a sense of great intelligence about her at the same time as a vagueness, an other-worldliness. We talked about what we were both doing, her adventures that week on local buses around Youth Hostels on the island. She told me how, by living in a retirement apartment in Edinburgh, she'd lost the stars in the night sky to a halo of orange security lighting. But in certain places, at night on Arthur's Seat, she could still find true dark, even in the City. She told me of her former love of walking, and we spoke of unconventional lifestyles.

I told her how a man at a similar table in a Glen Lyon café had said my lifestyle sounded like retirement, and how friends tell me I appear to be on holiday all the time whilst I feel I can never be 'on holiday'. My life is filled with vocation that has no nine-to-five, that is both play and work, that can never be put aside even in sleep, and whose grip on me I love and occasionally resent.

'People just think that it can only be work if it makes you miserable,' she said. 'Ignore it.' She seemed to understand with almost no explanation what I was doing and why.

During our conversation, it was as if a tide that had gone out came splashing and tumbling back onto the shore. My journey had been in question the night before, my way lost. I'd felt wounded and weak. Kindled by Philip Tordoff's blessing, and fed by 'High Pastures', my commitment was restored by meeting this woman.

When she stood up to catch her bus back to Uig, she paused, and made sure I was listening.

THE END

Sligachan
Inn

Cuillins

Bla Bheinn

blue
shed
cafe

bothy

Am Mam

Kilmarie

Loch
Slappin

Sea

Elgol

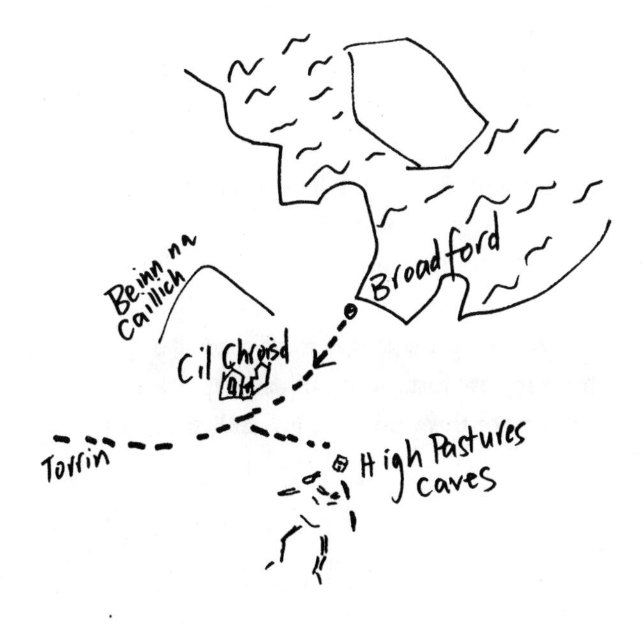

← Direction of travel
(3rd)

'I have arthritis now, it's stopped me. But please, keep doing it,' she said. 'Keep walking. For just as long as you can.'

And I promised her that I would.

I was rummaging in my rucksack outside the café when I heard the blue Highland bus growling up the hill behind me. I turned around. There was only one passenger on it, seated near the front. At the same moment, each of us threw an arm high in the air in an affectionate salute. I followed the bus with my eyes until it was out of sight.

In this brief meeting a connection seemed to have sprung between us. Perhaps I'd seen the woman I hope to be in my 70's and she'd seen someone she used to be. As she headed northeast past Cill Chriosd and up the valley to Broadford, I knew that a tall broad hill would watch the bus pass at its feet along the single track road. I began to understand that in her simplest form, the cailliche represents a different stage of life. I thought of this woman as my cailliche, and I no longer felt afraid.

The sun was forcing its way through gale-tossed cloud onto russet bands of seaweed when I descended to the shore of Loch Slapin from the Blue Shed Cafe. Preoccupied by this I barely noticed a grey car pass me in the opposite direction, then re-pass from behind and stop just ahead of me. Out of it burst Jane and Elaine. We greeted each other like long-lost friends. In fact we'd met only four days earlier in the bar of the Tomdoun Hotel, just west of Loch Garry on the Kinlochourn road.

I'd been only just on the right side of despair when I arrived. The only hour in which it hadn't rained in the previous two days had been the final one. I squelched into the bar where a fire was roaring, tea brewing and a game of Trivial Pursuit underway. I was grateful to be taken out of my solo reveries with maps and notebooks, to chat with fellow walkers Jane and Elaine from Brighton and a man from London, a private secretary to a junior minister at Westminster.

On another table behind me I heard a woman repeatedly ask her husband, 'Is it going to rain tomorrow?'

He deftly evaded an answer each time.

At last she became more determined, 'I have to know.'

'It's going to rain every day this week,' he replied wearily.

I tried not to hear him as I savoured my glass of red wine and took in the fire-warmed faces around me. It was almost as though, like people suffering war, a little adversity from the weather had created close kinship between otherwise diverse people. At moments such as these, regaining the mutual territory of humans seemed sweet.

So much seemed to have happened to me in the four day interlude since meeting Jane and Elaine – elation, cold, river crossings, emotional crossroads, seas. I'd resumed a steady path; I'd not gone home. But the interlude seemed to heighten the coincidence of our re-meeting. Seeing them again was a small joy that nourished my way ahead alone.

My journey took fifteen days. I passed through some of the most visited places in the Highlands – Glen Lyon and the Great Glen, and under the most climbed hills of Glencoe, Grey Corries, the Glenelg peninsula. Such was the conspiracy of route or time of year or weather that, with the obvious exception of the West Highland Way, I barely met a single walker on my route between days one and day fourteen.

'Weren't you lonely?' people often asked me.

Haldane refers to the drovers' special qualities of 'head, heart and body'. I like to think that the 'heart' was not just pulse and fitness but the love of the land and movement, of friendships springing from the special ways of path and road and journey, and that the 'heart' was also in the artistry of their markings on the land.

There's a different kind of loneliness that you confront on any walk in the Highlands. Just after crossing the river at the head of Glen Arnisdale at Glen Dubh Lochan, I passed through fragments of a village that was once a drovers' overnight stance. It would have been a beautiful place to live, on a slightly raised point above the bend in the river. A cluster of houses still stands there, one with a tree spraying up through its hearth. Its gables still stretch bravely skywards like two hands, but they hold no roof between them.

Passing sheilings reduced to tumbled stone and still surrounded by an oasis of green in the high glens, I sometimes fancy I glimpse faces from the corner of an eye, or catch the murmur of voices – curious at a traveller passing. But they don't discomfort me as the relics left from the deliberate clearance of people from the Highlands do, perhaps because sheilings were always intended to be temporary.

Much of the drovers' original route on Skye is now under tarmac - a testament to the 'truth' of their original line. On my long road walk between Broadford and Kilmarie, vehicles became an irritation, especially as the howling wind often drowned out the warning sounds of their approach. Builders' vans, delivery trucks, tourist cars. Had they no idea that this was an ancient right of way for feet, that my means of travel pre-dated theirs?

Crossing a narrow bridge near Faoilean on the west side of Loch Slapin, a large red pick-up roared towards me and showed no sign of slowing or allowing me time to get off the bridge. I flattened myself against the rails as the red-roar-chrome flashed past me. A Bruce Willis lookalike was braced at the wheel, avoiding eye contact. I scowled after his flashing progress under the hills at the head of the Loch, raised my arms and stick like a furious old lady, shouting, 'Don't mind me!'

Later, I wondered if I shouldn't be welcoming the traffic as the signature of new life in the Highland and Islands. Perhaps that stick-creature smugness wouldn't do.

At Kilmarie, three miles short of the end of the peninsula at Elgol, I turned onto an old path to Camasunary. A southerly wind had been scolding me all day and the hard road thudding up through my joints. It was late. As the path uncoiled its broad stone-paved assurance towards the low *bealach* at Am Mam, I was stung by hailstones. Looking back I saw the end of a rainbow rising from the path, arcing brightly against Loch Slapin and the shore and low hills of the Sleat peninsula beyond.

On the shoulder of Am Mam, water had collected in a level section of the path and was being whisked into small waves. Loose cords and straps on my clothing and rucksack whipped my skin. I might have been angered at this treatment. But then the first sight of the Cuillins sprang at me, growing above the near horizon with every further step. Dark cloud had lifted to sit just above the range, and the tops seemed to be reaching upwards, trying to claw it back. The summits, jagged and hooked, sparred in a line across my view.

The sight of this drove me forward until I could look down into the valley as well as up. I struggled to resist the wind; to stand and look. I gripped my camera, trying to hold it still against the wind-buffet. My hands trembled. Low sun, escaped from under the cloud, was crackling onto Loch Scavaig, sharpening the curved lines of waves sweeping onto the shore, the islands of Eigg and Rum floating shadows beyond. The broad, flat valley entrance of Camasunary was floodlit green. There was a small flash of whitewashed bothy.

On a flat rock I set up a precarious self-timed photo and stood in front of the vista. At one edge of the resulting picture, the mountains are blasted away in swathes of swirling white light. The darker suggestion of land creeps back at the other edge. The expression on the face in front of it is part triumph, part confusion. I seem caught in a whirlpool. And the face has a look borrowed from my father.

This place that I had pictured as a calm haven was ragged and tempestuous. Standing high above it, something pure and visceral touched me. It was as though body and soul had been streamlined by my simple journey. I'd carried all that I seemed to need for life on my back. I'd walked into a gathering state of intensity. The solitude, the physical stress, the hurdles overcome had tuned me emotionally for this chaffing and shaking by gale and mountain. A high drama hailed my journey's end with a storm-blaze of rock, air, water and fire.

When I brought to mind Turner's painting, *Loch Coruisk*, it shared my sense of the elemental fireworks of weather and the Cuillin, but the tiny figures he portrayed amidst it didn't seem to represent my own experience. This primal connection made me feel bigger, braver, more human. It was as if the wind had roared against me in my opened-up state and I'd responded with a blast of something deep and profound. I stood there and cried.

In the old days of the Sligachan Inn, climbers and walkers were confined to a small back room where you were lucky to get a packet of crisps. Now there's a huge purpose-built barn of a place with room for everyone. Food is served all day, so I celebrated with sticky toffee pudding and custard.

A man sat down at the next table to me. He was cycling between the Armadale ferry and his friend's house in Braes, up visiting from Cumbria. We exchanged anecdotes of Fisherfield Forest, lightweight tents, days spent in mountains. We left each other after a frenzy of chatter in stunned smiles at the sheer joy of being able to have such adventures.

On the main road north, a modern day droving spectacle drew drinkers to the windows. Two enormous lorries, herded by police escort were carrying parts of a wind turbine north. Slowed to a crawl by the hill up from Sligachan, they trailed long lines of traffic behind.

'Fucking irresponsible,' said the barman. 'Why don't they take them through at 3 am?'

The previous day the main road north had been closed for several hours when one of the lorries had fallen off it.

Pushed to the back of my mind while I ate my pudding and drank tea, was the realisation that I had no idea what I was going to do next. Waiting for the bus to Portree was a way of suspending a decision further. It wasn't long before a car pulled up and I was being offered a lift by a couple who had been at the Inn. In the brief journey I learnt something of their lives and history with this island, and of their day battling with the wind on Bla Bheinn, isolated from each other by speech-ripping wind that imprisoned them in their cagoule hoods.

The line of this walk had linked places and people warm in my affection from a twenty-five year relationship with this part of Scotland. I'd teased up memories of past climbs, pub nights, days spent with friends and lovers. I hadn't planned the route around this, at least not knowingly, but now I see it as a string upon which the jewels of special moments are held in lapidary brightness.

Ben Okri talks about the process of writing as dropping a line into the unconscious and seeing what comes up. Mine was a different sort of line, and yet my path had this hidden, underwater, underworld quality. I didn't know what would bite, come bobbing to the surface along the line.

I longed to maintain this simplicity for a little longer, to keep walking, even to turn around and walk back again, arriving at my front door a month after I'd left. The trees I passed in Glen Lyon would then have been toasted and bronzed with the change of season rather then just golden and copper-crowned as they were.

It took me seven hours to reach home from Portree, even with the vagaries of buses and hitchhiking; less than thirty minutes for every day I'd walked. Teased by glimpses of places I'd passed, it felt like a betrayal and leaving my line after fifteen days brought a bruise of loss.

The walk traversed a space 'inbetween'. There were thresholds, an equinox, caves, shores, bogs, bridges, tidal flats, roadside hostelries – liminal places which can be turning points or transitions; places where normal limits don't apply. I'd walked with the gods and with the dogs. It had been a period out of my normal life. And yet it had also been an intense period of my life. I'd set out to follow an old droving trail but I had also opened up some buried chambers inside myself and the walk had given me time to dwell on their contents.

Back at home, I had little idea how to absorb the lessons into my everyday life, but the walk had identified one important task.

Not long after my return I went to meet Lewis Jarvis in Edinburgh. He had an old man's baby face, a double chin and Andean-sloped eyes. He was truly a child of the mountains. From out of their drawer the day before, I'd taken the pair of red and yellow leather boots made by Jonti twenty-five years before. They were both strange and familiar to hold after all those years growing more precious in the dark. Now they belong to Lewis. Whether they will be practical footwear for a baby I doubt, but it seemed appropriate for this special child born in the betwixt and between of the year, that they should be his.

Walking Home

Château de Lavigny, Switzerland, September 2012

After nearly three weeks, I feel at home here, my daily rhythms well-established, the immediate area familiar enough to settle me. The temperature has dropped from the 33 degrees of my arrival to around 15, making me feel I've lived through a whole season. And indeed, September brought in several days of high winds which shook the plane tree into a sea-storm of sound and greenery outside the window.

When I stepped out this morning, the grass was dew-soaked and the air sweetly cool before the sun rose above mist. The lower lawn was freshly mowed, conjuring with its scent my childhood garden as well as reasserting the ghost-lines of the Rowohlt's former swimming pool. Their place of play and laughter, I imagine.

I start to mourn in anticipation, packing up memories of the morning walks I've designed for myself whilst here so that each one beats with a new poignancy as I follow it for the last time. The trees in the arboretum are crowned golden when I walk there now, and the wind scuttles dry leaves along the paths. Grapes will be harvested soon; sheep and cattle brought down from the mountains; and on the Lake, I see the yachts taking part in a regatta heel over, their sailors padded with clothing. On many days the French Alps across the water are bundled in cloud but on one day of special clarity, Mont Blanc finally reared up; higher, whiter, more sharply sculpted than the serrated skyline.

From my desk I see the Manager's eight year old daughter Tatiana, running across the lawn in red shoes with her hair streaming behind, calling for the cat 'Mimi'. She seems to skip with the carefree charm of the place and with my sense of loss: The flick of lizards' tails on the garden wall when I pause for lunch; the vineyard stripes leading my eye away from the Château towards the Aubonne river; the laughter of my fellow writers echoing between yellow-painted walls. By weaving our storylines through these rooms, mingling with words left by others, and by gathering to share food and conversation as the light slips from the garden and the Lake, we've made a home of it. It's tempting to wonder whether I'll 'double back' one day to collect the memories of this special time and place.

I've always drawn my spirituality from turns in the seasons, and usually pause for reflection or celebration at the solstices and equinoxes, full moons or other cosmic events.

I remember one Easter early in primary school when the story of Jesus, his life, death and rebirth, made an ecstatic impact on me. It was connected to singing the hymn, 'There is a green hill far away'. I imagined a dome-shaped mound of fairy-tale eccentricity with a wooden cross on its summit such as, for example, the one we often climbed as a family at West Wycombe, crowned with a mausoleum. The next line always foxed me – why would a green hill need a city wall? – but I ignored that. I remember standing in the school playground thrilling at a mystical cycle represented by a green hill. I was disappointed that I never quite recaptured the feeling at subsequent Easters, but the sense of a turning year marked with seasonal beacons never left me.

These days I find myself drawn to the lives of the early Saints, men who seem spiritual 'vagabonds', who walked huge distances sowing religious ideas as they went, and whose earthiness forges a humble connection to the sacred. Last year a small commission from the National Museum of Scotland sent me stomping about on Saint Fillan's ways in west Perthshire in order to write about one of his relics, a crozier handle said to cure cattle. This summer I walked from Inverness to Tain, emulating ancient pilgrims to Saint Duthus' shrine. And here, my morning walk frequently takes me through the village of Saint Livres (not, disappointingly, named after a saint of books, but a corruption of Saint Libere or Liberius).

In the first of these final two walks I follow Saint Cuthbert's Way in the border country between Scotland and England, from Melrose Abbey to Lindisfarne (or Holy Island). In the second I take the hour-long circuit around the Birks of Aberfeldy from my home.

It's a common experience for walking to bring a spiritual peace, a sense of 'home' or connection with places, nature, people, as well as offering excitement or enchantment. These are slow ways, with possibilities for stillness and reflection, qualities I associate with the melancholy acceptance of Autumn.

This project, this retreading of former ways first with feet and then in words has left me with traces of red dust, glacier ice, granite, in my veins, and a spring in my step. I've beaten the bounds of things I half know, uncovered history and inhabited my wild, childish self again, to relive the thrill of being drawn into a landscape, connecting to nature, seeing where a way leads and who or what I meet. I've appreciated better the various motives of footfall and made peace with the contradictory impulses of familiarity and 'otherness'; self-sufficiency and company. And there's a sense now that, as well as doubling back, walking moves me forward into some new terrain.

To be a pilgrim

N

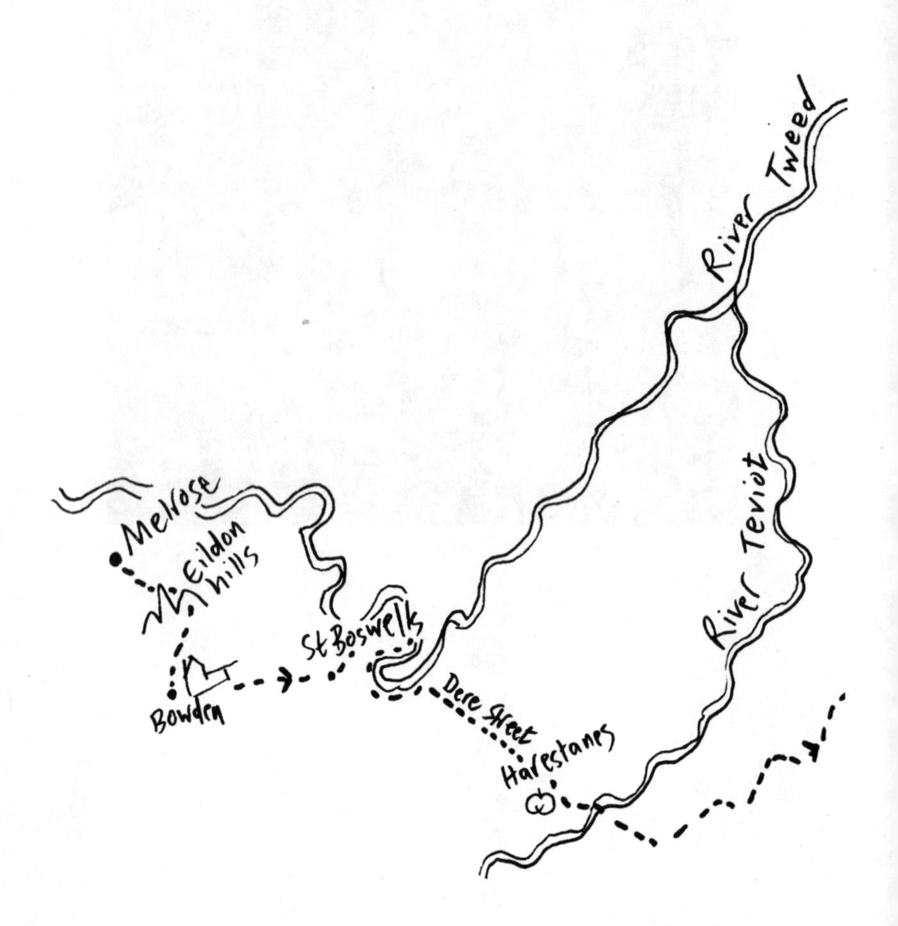
River Tweed
River Teviot
Melrose
Eildon hills
Bowden
St Boswells
Dere Street
Harestanes

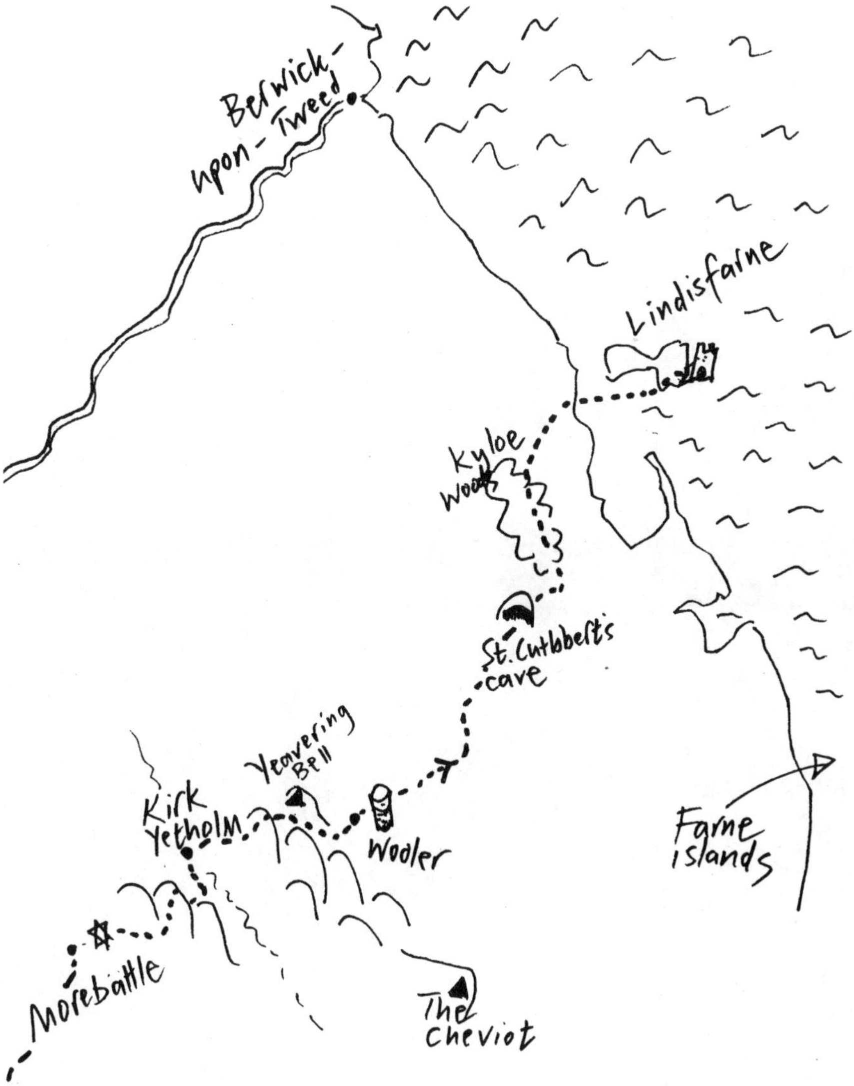

Berwick-upon-Tweed

Lindisfarne

Kyloe wood

St. Cuthbert's cave

Yeavering Bell

Kirk Yetholm

Wooler

Farne islands

Morebattle

The Cheviot

Saint Cuthbert's Way
Melrose to Lindisfarne

Bring me my scallop shell of quiet
From *The Passionate Man's Pilgrimage,* Sir Walter Raleigh

Up we went, luxuriating our boots and trouser legs in the deep pink, skitey mud. Up and out of Melrose, in time for the shock of shower and rainbow on the northern summit of the Eildon hills. The landscape spread itself like a map. To the east was the first chapter of the five-day walk that Phil and I had planned. It would be defined by the movements of Saint Cuthbert's life as shepherd, monk, hermit, and Bishop of Lindisfarne, between the Roxburghshire plains and the tern-screeched islands of the east. The Cheviots rose between the two, blocking our view to the coast.

Weather came at us from the west. Flashes of sun scratched bright the wide ribbon of the Tweed winding between the towns and villages of the first day's route and illuminated to the northeast the site of the Roman fort, Trimontium. River crossings there ghost through two millennia alongside the A68 flyover: Leaderfoot Viaduct, Dry Grange Bridge, Fly-boat Brae ferry, the long-gone Roman bridge.

On this hilltop, made something of by both Bronze Age and Roman peoples, I took out a guide book and read a story to Phil.

It was here, according to a Border Ballad, that 13th century poet

Thomas the Rhymer kissed and was led away by the Fairy Queen. Three ways presented themselves: a narrow thorny way of righteousness; a broad way of wickedness; and a winding way, the third, down a 'fernie brae'. This takes Thomas on an extraordinary journey through the 'mirk, mirk night', wading crimson streams into elfland, into a fertile garden beneath these hills. There the Queen plucked and offered him a red apple.

'They do that, don't they?' Phil said.

'Who?'

'Women in myths. Offering apples all over the place. Getting men into trouble.'

The Fairy Queen promised the apple would give Thomas 'a tongue that can never lie'. He tried to resist this gift, but her charms seem to have won the day. She only kept him there for seven years, then released him back to the mortal world to become 'True Thomas', famous for his prophecies.

We were just one hour into our 62 mile journey, and were already excavating stories from the volcanic core of this trio of hills which stand proud of the surrounding lowlands weathered down over millennia.

A grey curtain sliced wind and hail between us and the Cheviots.

'Shouldn't we be getting on?' I said. My hands were cold and I was looking at my watch.

'What's the rush?' said Phil, getting out his camera.

For Phil, walking through the borderlands to the Northumberland coast represented a walk 'home'. A native of Newcastle and descended from the Eliot family, famous border 'reivers', he was passionate about Northumberland's castles and the ghost stories still creaking amongst their old stones. As a teenager he'd learnt to dive around the Farne islands, an experience which both opened him to the mysteries of an underwater world and to the world beyond. A few years later he bought a boat and chugged it north around the coast to Oban where he became a diver for clams, or scallops, and gradually made a career as a professional diver on civil engineering jobs. He didn't return home, settled instead on the Isle of Mull, walling himself into a cottage with books and warming it with log fires. He stepped away from his romance with the Northumbrian coast into the west and the Atlantic. But now, in his late forties, he had a longing to be back on those windswept eastern coasts.

Our final objective of Holy Island, or Lindisfarne, had been his destination from Newcastle for teenage expeditions where he and his brothers beat the locals at pool in the pub and then slept out amidst the dunes. Then there were more spiritual pilgrimages in later years and it became one of the places he was drawn to for peace and contemplation.

We were walking just before the clocks changed in late October. I felt a need to refresh my body with physical movement, to feel the spark of sun and rush of wind on my skin before giving in to the dark; to walk the length of the daylight hours. But I was less sure of the landscape and the destination, the path safely way-marked with Celtic crosses that would lead us without any need to navigate.

Phil and I had met only ten months before and this was our first long walk together. We were still adjusting to each other's pace, learning each other's territory. Although we'd already enjoyed exploring history embedded in landscape together, he with his cameras, and me with my sketchbook or words, our approach to life more generally was quite different. Whereas mine often seems shaped by the need for activity and achievement, to cross things off mental lists, Phil is an expert at 'being'. He's content in an armchair or warm hilltop with a book, or just savouring his own thoughts, as long as a cup of tea is to hand. If Newcastle are playing at St James' Park, or Kauto Star is running at Ascot he's excitable, and probably still not beyond throwing a punch in a pub if he sees the need. But beyond his slightly piratical non-conformity and the scent of the sea that came with him, it was his calm which attracted me to him. An antidote to my own rush.

'You're too hard on yourself,' he said, when I reflected that this was the first time I'd walked with a bed booked for each night, meals cooked for me, and no need to carry more than a change of clothes and snacks for the way. Of all the long walks I'd taken, this one felt most like a holiday.

I was walking away from my mountains and Highlands towards a flat coast and I wondered if I'd find it all too tame. Would something softer, gentler, something easier, still bring rewards?

In a sense, any long walk is a pilgrimage, a 'holiday' (or holy day) from familiar places and routines, and from possessions. A simple journey with an ultimate goal holds a bud of transformation, a means of renewing lost parts of ourselves. The pilgrim's goal has a similar focus to the mountaineer's summit, but it's steadier, quieter.

A pilgrimage can take many forms. It can be a social, noisy time, generating new stories and celebrations, as medieval ones famously did. Or it can be an individual setting themselves against challenges in the spirit of John Bunyan's Christian in *The Pilgrim's Progress*, who leaves behind family and home in order to arrive at the Celestial City. His 'wicket gate' is a portal between civilisation and a kind of wilderness, his journey evoking landscape archetypes : rivers to cross, paths, forests and plains stretching to faraway mountains that must later be traversed.

After the gate, Christian, just like Thomas the Rhymer, faces a forking of the way into three paths. He takes the hill called Difficulty, while his two colleagues choose the seemingly easier Danger and Destruction with obvious results. Despite its one-dimensionality, this mix of bible story, fairy tale, and hard journey rolling out across diverse landscapes captivated my imagination as a child, lasting way beyond primary school assemblies. The place names made pictures in my mind: The Slough of Despond; Doubting Castle; the Delectable

Mountains where Christian and his new friend Hopeful eat freely from orchards and vineyards, but where they're also given a glimpse of a smoky place that smells of brimstone.

The accumulated sense of quest, the journey through life that each of us walk in our own small allegory, the stripped down hardship of the 'hermit's' existence, eventually had me reaching for my walking boots so that I could physically inhabit such a purpose myself.

I wasn't walking Saint Cuthbert's way for religious reasons, and yet I love the stories of many traditions, and hoped to find some of these underfoot and to discover places that beat with a spiritual pulse I could connect to. In a curious way I realised that setting out on a journey, leaving home, also gives me a sense of 'coming home'. The dropping away of anxiety and everyday concerns results in a feeling of just being 'me'.

In another hour a copper track of dead leaf was winding us through beech tree and bracken.

'Mirk, mirk wood', I said, conflating Thomas and Tolkein.

Then we descended through Bowden village to its church, leafily embedded next to a burn. Sunshine stretched long autumn shadows across the graveyard with its hourglasses, angels and memorials to people who had lived and died nearby, or who travelled from here to live and die in far off places.

Inside, I was drawn to the seventeenth century Laird's Loft, a sort of theatre box of dark wood elevated on legs. On its central panel, the Ker family coat of arms in red and gold comprised stars and a crescent moon, billowing plumes of feather, and at its crown, a stag's head. At the centre of every other panel, a gold five-pointed star was painted, edged in red. Under each of the stars on a ledge running below the panels, someone had placed a single ripe red apple.

For me, the naïve style of the painting and the offering of apples struck a pagan chord – a natural magic, an earthy offering to the gods. However, underneath the apple ledge, an open hand and an axe framed these words of warning:

'Behold the axe lyes at the trees' root
To hew downe those that brings not forth good fruit
And when they'r cut the Lord unto his ire
Will them destroy and cast into fire.'

An angry god. A whiff of brimstone. One bad apple...

We arrived at Harestanes Visitor Centre the next morning looking for coffee. We'd reached it on a march of an hour and a half along a broad, straight Roman Road: Dere Street. Standing sentry along the way were high pillars of oak and beech with gnarly toes stretching down into the soil. The words, 'though he with giants fight,' strode into my mind and John Bunyan was stamping along with me:

'He who would valiant be 'gainst all disaster,
Let him in constancy follow the Master.
There's no discouragement shall make him once relent
His first avowed intent to be a pilgrim.'

The Fairy Queen had warned Thomas that the broad straight road is the road of wickedness. This one built by the Romans had led us to our Sunday worship, our celebration. 'BOG APPLE DAY', the sign proclaimed. I'd never heard of 'bog apples' before, but with caffeine, the mists cleared. Amongst the wind-tossed stalls of produce from the Borders Organic Group (BOG), we discovered apple and cinnamon scones that were rich and filling, spicy and buttered. Perhaps this could be construed as wickedness.

Then our way was rising with the further march of Dere Street, bridging the River Teviot and crossing the undulating plains towards the Cheviots. I began to feel I was in Berkshire with chalky dry ridge-ways dog-legging through bright cloisters of beech. In the last blast of the year's light, the air became clear and cold. The sun flushed up colour. Hedges rose as vermilion walls where hawthorn berries bubbled over them. The last rascally heads of elderberries glistened darkly from bare stems already de-leafed by wind. As we gained height, we began to feel the snarl of the westerlies licking around our ankles and necks from behind. St Cuthbert's beloved high, rugged places sharpened in the hills ahead of us and we tried to see where our route would penetrate them.

At Morebattle we took refuge in the Templehall Hotel, comforted by steak pie and gorgonzola risotto in the warm bar. Outside, the umbrellas of the summer's remnant beer tables had been felled and lay flapping on the ground like tattered, dying crows. The hotel's sign swung above the street and creaked back and forth its six-pointed gold star.

Phil lay on the bed after supper, cup of tea in hand, the storm-song outside all the entertainment he needed.

Cuthbert's defining experience happened on a night watching sheep, when he had a vision of lights descending to earth and then rising again, illuminating the whole sky towards Lindisfarne. News reached him the next day that Aidan had died at the time of his vision. Aidan was first Bishop of Lindisfarne and had been an early Irish monk at Iona responsible for Christianising Northumbria. Cuthbert knew he'd been called, and took himself firstly to a cave to reflect and then to the monastery at Melrose.

Cuthbert was torn between duty and the hermit's life, between island and high hilltop. He chose to walk everywhere as Aidan had done, in the spirit of democracy, talking to everyone he met. He also taught as he walked, reciting psalms or speaking of the patterns of the stars or plant lore. Bede tells how Cuthbert often took long journeys without carrying food, entrusting himself to God, the land or to fasting. But miracle-gifts came to him in the form of a fish delivered from an eagle's beak; fresh bread and meat nudged by a horse from the roof of a bothy while he prayed; dolphin flesh mysteriously delivered when he and two others were snowbound on a Scottish coast.

After twelve years as Prior on Lindisfarne, he left to become a hermit on the nearby island of Inner Farne (later agreeing to return to Lindisfarne as Bishop). As a hermit, he lived in near solitude, a simplicity in which he drew heaven and earth close to each other from a beehive-shaped cell. The word 'cell' makes me think of prison. And yet it's related to the 'clam' and its secrets, and to 'nest'. I like to visualise a hermit's refuge as a shell, rough cast on the outside, but lit with a pearly glow within and redolent of mysterious chambers and spirals of retreat. Home, protection and a place in which to grow. Later it was another type of shell, his coffin, in which Cuthbert's body, uncorrupted for several centuries, was carried between places out of reach of Viking raiders.

In the dark interior of Morebattle Church the next morning, stained glass colluded with sunlight to project an image of a shepherd wearing pilgrimesque sandals, and the words: 'the good shepherd giveth his life for the sheep.'

Bunyan had his pilgrims stopping to talk with shepherds in the final stages of *The Pilgrim's Progress*, 'leaning upon their staves as is common with weary pilgrims when they stand to talk with any on the way'. The shepherds, named Knowledge, Experience, Watchful and Sincere, pointed beyond the mountains to the Celestial City, leaving the pilgrims singing as they went on their way:

'Thus by the shepherds, secrets are reveal'd,
Which from all other men are kept conceal'd,

Come to the shepherds then, if you would see,
Things deep, things hid, and that mysterious be.'

Along our own way through the hills we often watched shepherd-farmers transforming individual sheep into liquid flocks, pouring them through a gateway or pooling them into a field corner. Their tools were quad bikes and collie dogs. Crooks, staves, staffs, croziers seemed to have been abandoned, but we leant on our walking poles as we watched them work their magic.

Phil, as usual, was ready to stop for a sight like this, perhaps to photograph it. He didn't worry about time and 'getting on'. We were using our feet to explore; to digress for a ruined house or linger over the colour of a beetle. The pause was as important as the pacing.

Farmland and its neat definitions gave way to the whip and wind-gutter of moor-grass as we climbed onto Wideopen Hill, our halfway point, our highest point. Deeper into the Cheviots, sunlight glanced into misted valleys, kissing them luminous green. The promise of hill upon hill, each a faded version of the former, stretched away into England. A dry stone dyke wormed, as integral as a spinal cord to each roll and curl of Crookedshaws Hill. It dropped north to the Bowmont valley which carries a river between the two villages of Town and Kirk Yetholm, the easterly of which was our stop for the night.

Kirk Yetholm was once home to a sizeable community of travelling people. As if medieval pilgrims, they set out from the church at the start of each season on the road. But unlike pilgrims, the motion that has defined the lifestyle of Gypsies and the Scottish Travelling Folk has sometimes seemed a threat to settled people. Their fate was in some periods vastly different according to which side of the border they were on, but execution, outlaw, or blame for acts of crime have dogged them through centuries. We saw little sign of them, except for some old photos in the 'Border' pub, hung as if a curiosity, a people made exotic by the passing of time and presumably by their absence.

The next day we climbed to the border into England at Eccles Cairn, and the Eildons showed themselves behind us for the last time. By then they were a shadow in distant mists that required screwed-up eyes. As we turned to commit ourselves fully to the valleys and muscular bare hills between ourselves and the coast, they flickered their last fairy dance, and disappeared over the horizon.

Northumbrian names took flight from the map as we neared them, enjoyable to say aloud:

'Coldburn Hill,' I said.

'Sticky Bog,' Phil replied.

'Hedgehope Hill.'

'Foulburn Gair.'

'Skirl Naked,' I snarled in conclusion.

Kissing gates disappeared for a day and we walked in near silence, each taking our own inner way, yards apart. Hillsides were toasted with bracken, rippled by wind and sun. Yeavering Bell – the goat hill and hill fort – passed to our left with its high necklace of rock ramparts. Humbleton Hill brought Harry Hotspur's name, in his decisive battle there against the Scots, to our lips. Across the high plateau we were blown on old wide tracks, which seemed articulate and alive in their carrying of us, allowing us freedom to look around. The first glimpse of the sea stopped us to gaze.

Then down we went into Wooler, where Theakstons beer was on tap by a cosy fireside.

In the early afternoon of the next day, the path brought us along a processional aisle of Scots Pine to an overhanging rock: St Cuthbert's Cave. Crosses fashioned from sticks and grass had been left here; names carved into soft rock over several centuries. We sat in the sunshine and made tea, enjoying moments of peace and warmth.

'I never want to get in my car again,' Phil said, and we tried to imagine a year of walking everywhere we wanted to go. It brought about a diminishing of horizons, a clarifying of priorities.

Just beyond the cave, on the brow between Greensheen Hill and

Cockenheugh, a gateway offered the first glimpse of our destination. John Bunyan's shepherds took the pilgrims to the top of a high hill called Clear to show them the Celestial Gates through a 'perspective-glass'. The view was blurred by their shaking hands, but they still saw 'something of the glory of the place'.

Through binoculars we admired a curved blue horizon along which lay the pale promontory of Lindisfarne, a crescent shaped spike of land moored to the mainland by a cord of sand. On an outcrop of rock at its southerly tip a fairy-tale castle grew like an upright winkle shell.

We pressed on, looking out to the Farne islands as we walked. It was amongst these stepping-stones in the North Sea, under the gaze of 'Grace Darling's' lighthouse, that Phil had learnt to dive when he was sixteen.

I imagined Cuthbert alone on his island hermitage, seabirds wheeling around his head, otters at his feet. Under his hand were the black and white 'cuddy' ducks, or eiders, who adopted his name.

In the late afternoon, violet shadows laid lines along the stubble of the coastal farmland. A tractor towed behind it a dark wake of soil and a white, airborne flock of cries. A short-eared owl watched from a post as we stepped barefoot onto the low-tide flats, onto mud that was tangy with salt and something burnt-smelling and ancient, that sucked onto the skin, dyeing it with dark grazes that later resisted soap.

A cacophony of godwits, curlews, sandpipers, took my hand to the book of 'Scottish Birds'.

'How do the birds know whether they're Scottish or not?' asked Phil.

Birds from across the world are welcomed by this unique terrain to over-winter here or stop on their journeys south or west. They belong for the length of their stay, paying no heed to borders and not judged ill for their need to move on, or their transience.

We intended to take the 11th century pilgrims' route that cuts the corner of the tarmac causeway making it four or five miles across the mudflats. Cuthbert came the same way on his first journey here, choosing foot rather than horseback in order to give himself time for prayer and reflection. Tourist literature cautions newcomers to seek local knowledge: 'Never attempt this route at dusk or on a rising tide!' We were attempting it on the verge of both.

As we left true land behind, we started to cross a wilderness of horizontals – buff and slime-green beneath our feet, a lilac sky above – a journey of over an hour following a line of barnacle-crusted vertical posts doubled in height by their reflection on wet sand. Our own reflections had us walking on water.

It seemed we were entering Cuthbert's domain where polarities evoke his dilemma between solitude and public calling. It's neither quite land, nor quite sea, can be a place of in or out-tide, of seals grounded or swimming, of stalking birds that can wade or fly or float. A place for shellfish that are half-fish, half-flesh; half-stone, half-living-thing. The contradictions are separated by only the most fragile veil or transformed from one to the other by a slice of the clock face.

It's not difficult to feel you're in a sacred place.

Geese had been squabbling in a party behind us, unseen. Then a change in pitch made me look behind and I saw them rise to form a serpent of dark flecks across the sky, breaking into branches from a central spine as they flew away. As they settled into flight and ordered themselves, the lines looked like sentences of text that had broken free from a script, each sentence curling away independently, but still holding as one central body; a scattered page. A little later, one bird returned – a croak of complaint escaping with every wing-beat – on some unexplained, solitary, mission.

A moan rose in the gloom ahead of us, then a wail and a whimper, as the small dark outline of St Cuthbert's Isle emerged to our right. The voices grew louder and more numerous, until it seemed that a mournful seal-song was guiding us in, or perhaps a siren-song was luring us out towards the rushing tongue of tide that forced us to detour from the marked way. This press of adventure, the rapid change of time and tide held us in a betwixt-and-between world within the dim sight of our destination, within a breath of a pilgrimage fulfilled.

The colour of the mud beneath our feet gradually deepened to match the sky, and we steered ourselves towards a narrow spit of sand-land between the two lilacs. Distant-looking in the dusk, the southerly end of the land had started to prickle with artificial light. At its tip rose the blunt bluff of castle. But we didn't fully realise how night had taken charge until we were winding amongst lit windows through the empty stone streets of the village towards our final stop, The Crown and Anchor. It was as if we'd reached the still centre of a labyrinth; circled a spiral staircase within a seashell. We'd fallen into step. The romance of place was now shared.

Behind us, the world had turned to monochrome. The sea washed away our footsteps and cast Lindisfarne off to become an island sanctuary again, a lulled cradle. Tide and the night stopped our feet, halted the onward rhythm of our journey. We had arrived, and the place insisted that we rest a day or two before we go on our way again.

Friendly Paths

The hills
Moness burn
THE TOWN
home

URLAR FARM

The West

River Tay

The Birks of Aberfeldy, Perthshire Scotland

One never reaches home, but wherever friendly paths intersect the whole world looks like home for a time.

Hermann Hesse, from *Demian: The Story of Emil Sinclair's Youth,* 1919

The burn cackles, calling walkers to follow it upstream. And, as usual, I submit to the deep embrace of the wooded gorge. For a change, I head for the bridge, to take the path up the eastern side where I haven't been for some days.

This is 'The Birks of Aberfeldy', where trees brim from a cleft in the hillside and a burn plummets down its centre from the Falls of Moness. It's a chink of arcadia fashioned from water, woodland and rock, made famous by Rabbie Burns' song that's preserved it as a pleasure walk, an up-one-side-down-the-other walk, for over 200 years. Next year has been declared a year of 'Homecoming' by the Scottish government, celebrating the 250th anniversary of the national bard. One of the new signs erected in the car park shows him looking rather elegant, rather 'stuffed-shirt' for one born in a snowdrift and said to enjoy a roll in the heather.

But the walk is still 'The Birks' in any year and in this flamboyant Autumn season it's particularly popular, an hour-long pilgrimage shared by locals and visitors with dogs and children. First-timers found panting towards the top ask walkers striding down, 'Is it much further?' Like a church or shrine, it reassures us where we belong; it's a rural promenade in which we show ourselves to each other.

I came to live here in 1995 for a job with WWF Scotland. When I left in 2002 to pursue a freelance life through writing, there seemed no reason to move. It's a small town of only about 2,000 people at the heart of Scotland, and I had found many friends here, a wonderful independent bookshop 'the Aberfeldy Watermill', a mountainous landscape, and a gradual sense, through familiarity, of this being 'home'.

I've walked The Birks often, in many seasons and weathers, even at night. The way responds generously to my habit, offering words or images when I'm stuck for them, or the gift of a change in mood. It airs my mind and exercises my body when it's cramped and subdued by work. I walk it with friends too, visitors or local people. I'm never bored by it, and can always vary the route slightly; descending by a different track or exploring further up the hill beyond the Falls. Sometimes I leave the etched ways and follow fainter, incipient paths, just to see where they go. They might dump me in bog or snaring heather but I like the deviation; the combination of heartily sharing the ground and absconding to the margins.

Returning home after a period away, this walk's one of the first things I'll do. I re-learn the land with my repeated steps, my circuits. But it's not static. Things happen. Each time there's the possibility of new discoveries. And I might meet someone by chance who's taking their own turn of The Birks. Karen perhaps, coming the other way with at least two dogs, reading as she goes. We might stand chatting on the path for 15 minutes; the only place we tend to see each other. Or the fit-looking couple in their early seventies who pound up and plummet down daily. We always exchange greetings and grins of recognition even though I don't know their names.

By keeping the paths beaten, our feet earn us the right to be here. We recognise each other as those who beat the bounds with a quotidian rhythm. We're like a 'hefted' flock of sheep with a mental map of their territory, a memory that apparently lasts at least three generations. We're not contained by fences and perimeters, but share alliance to the path.

'Birks', the Scots word for 'birches', seems inaccurate at the beginning of the walk because I reach the bridge through a grand hall of beech. A copper carpet winds between dark trunks sheathed in luminous moss, the most figure hugging of cocktail dresses. Ahead, between these dark pillars, gold leaves blaze, dazzling between bare branches like panes of stained glass.

When I reach the centre of the bridge something breaks my foot-rhythm, a splinter shears through the familiar. Incongruous against the russet foliage, two white roses have been left balanced on the hand rail. Wrapped in white ribbon, in a bouquet with some sword-long leaves, they're not fastened to the rail. At any moment they might be tossed by a breeze into the hands of white-water bridesmaids below.

I don't know why they're there.

The burn flowing under the bridge has a floor of peat-washed pebbles, and is latticed above by fallen trees that the moist air has helped colonise with creeping moss, tongues of fern. Robert Burns' song recalls it as a 'foaming stream'.

I look again at the white roses and wonder at their story. Do I know why they're there? I recall now something I was told a night or two ago.

Since I've lived here, I've known of two men who've fallen, slipped into the gorge. Both were rescued. Even a dog abandoned with a broken leg was carried out a day later down the slip of precipice and moss. But this man was determined, lost amidst the Burnsian braes, on everyone's favourite walk. Perhaps it was his own favourite once. His body was found hanging from a tree by a jogger one recent morning: a failed marriage the rumour.

A path of deep leaves leads me away from the bridge and the strangeness of the roses. I'm a child again, shuffling my feet and flicking and scuffing; airy play that reveals a dark under-layer of last autumn's crumbling mould. Beneath that, and beneath that, it's stored in damp-scented archives, year upon year.

In a copper-floored clearing, there's another surprise for my walk today: a pale timber bench that I've never seen before. A dull brown figure sits on it with his back to me. Four people are crowding him with a camera on a tripod. One man stands behind the figure, leans a hand on the shoulder, looking into a lens.

Now I see who the figure is. Our national poet. Or perhaps I shouldn't say 'our'. As an incomer, a 'white settler', his language isn't quite mine, even though I love Scots words like 'bahoochie', the part of the body that he's sitting on, and 'gloaming', 'wabbit', 'scrieve', 'stravaig'. Once the words are tasted on the tongue, I suppose they become my own.

I'm not the only incomer to these woodlands. Another new sign in the car park reminded me that non-native trees growing there were brought to the area by Perthshire's plant-hunters, Archibald Menzies and David Douglas in the 19th century, and more recently by Bobby Masterton. Decorating the parking area are Tibetan cherry, Japanese maple, western hemlock. Some of the words connected to plant introduction make me uneasy: 'alien', 'native', 'naturalised', 'exotic'. It's as if they're labels for some kind of judgement on the trees' right to remain. How long does a species need to be resident before it's granted citizenship anyway?

The poet is very absorbed, writing in his small notebook, face turned up towards the dancing light. A plaque on a rock further up the gorge already shows where he sat in 1787 to compose his song (or perhaps, as some would say, to adapt one he'd collected from Abergeldie). I feel a prickle of annoyance that his physical presence now interrupts the walk when his words could be left to echo in our minds: 'while o'er their heads the hazels hing'. It seems only a skip away from flesh-and-blood celebrity and *Strictly Come Dancing*.

As the photographers move away, I get closer to the statue. Fake verdigris lines the bronze creases of his clothes and the wrinkles of skin on his fingers. In the fold of each elbow, a small pool of rainwater has collected and in each floats a leaf. They're beech, not birch.

It reminds me that Dorothy Wordsworth barely gave a mention to the birches when she walked all around this area with her brother. Earlier in the same tour, they'd paid a sad visit to Burns' grave following his death seven years before. She imagined some of the places he walked and caroused as they continued on their way north, and William composed a poem to his remaining sons, which I imagine she assisted with.

I like to picture her walking here, with her stooped gait and tanned face. Instead of the birches she remarked on the planted laburnums – introduced to Scotland in the late 16th century – with leaves, 'of a golden colour, and as lively as the yellow blossoms could have been in the spring... I do not think I ever saw any that were of so brilliant colours in their autumnal decay.' Dorothy's words haven't earned her a statue.

I finally meet the birches, a host of them on the rising ground to my left: straight, slim and tall, they are silent, and swaying slightly. Their foliage is all filigree and lace after the sturdiness of the beeches. Despite the discipline of their spacing, they're too elegant to be soldiers, more like maidens, or a choir perhaps, erect and waiting for the opening note. They trail tousled tresses that are pronounced as shivering gold by the blue sky behind.

The path and burn come level with each other again as the channel narrows and slows between moss-furred, dripping cliffs. This is the rich, green heart of The Birks. A torrent forges in from the main waterfall above and from another fall close on my left. But the deepness of the gully here brakes and lazes the flow. A skim of white froth circles languidly on the black surface, betraying no bottom. Looking two hundred feet up, I appreciate how darkly I'm enfolded. Up there is sun-topped foliage, breezy lightness. My climb to it begins now on wooden steps and bridges.

Two grey-haired ladies are coming down towards me, clicking their walking poles.

'Have you seen the squirrels?' the first asks, as if they perform in one troupe. She means the red ones, which are natural here and not yet too threatened by encroaching greys, but still a prized sight.

'I've never seen any on this side,' I tell her.

She assures me that she has, she normally does. She'll be a Moness timeshare resident, I think; week-long visitors disgorged from matching white cottages – faux-crofts on cut lawns – to parade around The Birks and become part of the turning community.

Stone steps twist up now, past the small falls, around switchbacks. The temperature rises as I leave the clammy cavern, the dark slot of rock and water, for the sky. The path becomes dry underfoot, speckled yellow with birch leaves.

Once breathing hard it's good to pause and look across to the other side of the gorge. A bare grey cliff drops vertically, then relents, allowing a slope for plants and trees to cling to again, the leaf-floor there sodden crimson. A pylon imposes on the cliff in a bracken-lined forest-break before its wires soar overhead to this side. Below it a young man in grey is standing, looking down the gorge, then moving upwards along the path on his side, flickering through the lace of foliage and tree trunk until it swallows him.

The sight of him brings an echo of the man who died. I have to let the sadness settle into place amongst the leaf mould, amidst the tumble of rock. It changes the place. The trail of it leads back under the dark arc of branches that stopped me earlier: two white roses.

There's a sense of things opening out now, a breeze in the face. I glance down the plunging gully on my right. Through lattices of tree tangle, rock and lichen-fingered branches, lies a glimpse of black water. It has drained from 2,000 or so feet through heather and peat, sluicing along the bedrock to thunder a white curtain to that dark pool below.

Four teenagers in T-shirts bound past me, and I circle after them towards the bridge, where we all lean a while on the wooden balustrade. The burn hurls itself over the edge, shooting out a horizontal plume before gravity pulls it vertical to plummet 200 hundred feet. A tree-trunk bisects the pool below, wedged there for at least 40 years, so say the locals.

I should have kept a note of all the people I've stood here with, watching. I could make it an artwork like Tracey Emin's and call it *Everyone I have ever leant with, 1995-2008*.

I leave the bridge for a less-used path, guided by a line of yellow birch-leaves up through the woods. In summer this path is walled by head-high bracken, a passage through the young birch. Roe deer often flash between pale trunks. But now the bracken corridor is dying back and black stalks fall apart to widen the way for me.

The ground levels, I reach the road that carries on left up to Urlar Farm and right down to the town. The outline of Farragon Hill lies to the north, linking to the whole jagged Tairneachan Ridge that peeks through the birchy haze in fragments of grey-blue. In a month's time we'll be back to the bare skeletons of things, to walls of rock rather than these Japanese-print weeping birches whose yellow curtains steal the eye.

Crossing the road, a squealing gate leads to a plateau of grass and reeds and a path drops westwards. With the opening of the views to the surrounding hills, I sense my 'memory-markers' scattering the valley sides, linked by a web of paths. A picnic spot; a confession made over there; an illicit kiss here. High on the hillside opposite, a small white farmhouse perches on a green strip between dark forestry where David Robertson, a cheery sheep-farmer lived before leukaemia took him. At the bottom of the slope below me is the cottage I rented for two years with grotesquely patterned carpets, and piles of mice droppings. But my neighbours there have been a kind of yardstick to my years in this valley: the six-year-old now away in a hydro-electric engineering job, the white collie who arrived as an irrepressible puppy now taking every chance to lie down.

The writing of any story is mostly re-writing. My first draft will have a rough sense of direction and content, a provisional resolution, but then I'll revisit it again and again, re-seeing the material to tighten it, or even to allow it, if it insists, to follow a new route. I think of it as a repeated walk; a loop with varieties or diversions. Revisiting our own memories is like this too. We subtly reconstruct them as we go, so that our life stories are less like photographic, objective reality and more like an act of imagination, re-invented over and over. As Grace Paley says, 'When a story is told for the second time, it's fiction, no matter what'. Perhaps that's what makes remembering so pleasurable; it feels like a made-up story, complete with sensory detail and implied meaning.

On a walk like this made over many years, and on many occasions, I've cached so many memories amongst the rocks and trees and hills, that re-turning the walk also gives me a way of retracing my own story.

I love the feeling when all the uphill is done. The sweat cools, the hat goes back on, and my arms and legs swing with their new-found warmth and looseness. My feet know the way, leaving my mind to roam on its inner journey. When I'm alone this might be when body and mind collude with the path to prompt imagination or memory. But today, the rhythm has been jarred a little by white roses, and by statues.

Grass tufts up around cobbles, but my eyes reach for the far horizon, rest on the slopes where late afternoon sun toasts the bracken, setting off the white hilltops behind. It's the thrill of late October, when autumn and winter quiver together. The snow is down to about 2,000 feet. The fairy point of Schiehallion rises, insisting on its 500 million year presence; a tipping iceberg behind the dark forest on Dull Hill.

Walking away from the direction of home like this, the green road before me seems to promise a journey. Winds wash in, carrying a sea-scent of adventure, expedition, quest. From here I could just keep walking to Kenmore, Loch Tay, give in to the tidal tow of The West just as I did last September when I walked with the drovers' dogs through that chink of valley, over that low pass into the beyond, into landscapes over which I had no claim. Looking at these near hills and valleys since that journey, I feel for them a greater sense of affection and secret knowledge.

Thinking of the walk to Skye summons to my side the elderly woman to whom I made a promise. I will keep walking, and as yet nothing threatens, as arthritis has for her, to stop me.

And now my walking mind gives in to the familiar, agrees to close the circle as I turn, double back towards the town on a level road with views into the valley. Flat stubble fields stretch towards the hills on the north side of the valley at Weem, where Castle Menzies is tucked. The white of the cross on the hoisted Saltire flashes in the sun. Cars glisten east and west. Trees in Weem Woods are burnished red, and yellowing larch lies in broad strips higher up.

In the town lying below me like a plan, fine detail is carved by sun onto the clock face and the red belfry door on the church tower. Over the winding Tay arcs the bridge General Wade built in 1733, a strategic and rare crossing point built to quell an uprising. A pinch of blue river shivers in sunlight further east.

If I turn left when I reach Urlar Road, its steep tarmac will take me back to the town. I could instead choose the earthy snicket ahead, through the trees and down the steep bank to rejoin The Birks path. I could cross the bridge again, revisiting the two white roses shimmering against the dark gully of trees.

Perhaps next autumn when I cross the bridge, the date will be marked with some different flowers in an autumn colour. By then, the recollection of a stranger's death will have softened into my expectations of the walk, in the same way that I'll nod to the statue of Burns each time I pass, accepting him as a friendly landmark. With each turn of the circle, the walk revises itself; the archive deepens.

But now I look down on a field of grey slate roofs amongst which slopes my own. Contained within this walk each time I do it is the forever-pleasure of turning for home. At this point I always start to think ahead to putting on the kettle and making tea. Tomorrow perhaps I'll take a turn of the story once again.

Notes and Bibliography

Saunters

Page 11 The Château de Lavigny International Writers' Residence was founded by the late Jane Rowohlt in memory of her husband, the German publisher, Heinrich Maria Ledig-Rowohlt. Her wish was to bequeath their home, the Château de Lavigny, for a writers' residence offering and fostering 'a spirit of international community and creativity.' www.chateaudelavigny.ch

Page 12 Jean-Jacques Rousseau wrote in his *Confessions* (1782) that he could 'meditate only when I am walking. When I stop, I cease to think; my mind only works with my legs'.

For an exploration of how people at different life stages and in different cultures make 'spaces' into 'places', turning freedom into security and forming attachment to landscapes, Yi-Fu Tuan's book, *Space and Place – The Perspective of Experience* (University of Minnestota Press, 1977) is a fascinating read.

The Opening Door

Page 21 Claire Tomalin's biography *Thomas Hardy, The Time-Torn Man* (Penguin, 2007) was invaluable background reading for this chapter. In pages 33-4 the role of walking to the formation of the writer and the writing is described. I have quoted from pages 314 'Part of him was ecstatically absorbed in recalling…; 33 'learnt to read the noises of the fields…' and 'Walking the roads, meeting…'; xxiii 'an archaeologist uncovering objects…'

Page 23 The Penguin Classics (2005) edition of *A Pair of Blue Eyes* includes a preface written by Hardy in 1895 (pp 389-90) from which I took the quotation 'The place is pre-eminently …the region of dream and mystery…'etc. Further quotes from the text appear in this edition at pages 237, 'Bodily activity will…'; 274 'Elfride, I never saw such a sight…'; 59 'There far beneath and before them, lay…'; 216 'We colour according to our moods…'

Page 26 *Some Recollections* by Emma Hardy, Ed. Evelyn Hardy and Robert Gittings (Oxford University Press, 1961). 'Often we walked down the…'

Page 34 Carole Vincent is a Boscastle-based artist who works in concrete: www.carolevincent.org

Hardy's poems most connected with his first wife, Emma, and the Boscastle area can be found in *The Complete Poems,* Thomas Hardy (Macmillan 1976), many in the section 'Poems of 1912-13'. I have quoted from: *When I Set Out for Lyonesse, The Seven Times, She Opened the Door, Midnight on Beechen 187-, A Dream or No, Beeny Cliff, I Found Her Out There, The Phantom Horsewoman, The Haunter, A Dream or No.*

In the Footsteps of Thomas and Emma Hardy by Heulyn Lewis and Ginny Lewis (the North Cornwall Coast and Countryside Service, 2003) is an illustrated account of the couple's time in Cornwall and includes maps of the walks.

Dancing, kicking up her legs

Page 41 Jessie Kesson wrote monthly essays drawing on her experiences as a cottar's wife, 'Country Dweller's Year', for the *Scots Magazine* in 1946 under the pseudonym 'Ness MacDonald'. The epigram and my quotes: 'Spring there is more than colour…', 'you feel any moment…', and 'The smell of Spring in the hills…' come from April's essay. The essays are available to read now in *A Country Dweller's Years – Nature writings by Jessie Kesson*, Ed. Isobel Murray (Kennedy and Boyd, 2009).

Page 42 *Jessie Kesson – Writing her Life* is a wonderful biography by Isobel Murray (Canongate 2000). I have quoted from page 1 'a series of violent shifts…'; page 140 'a 'tornado' at nineteen …'is there no settle in you?". Alastair Scott's description of her as a 'one woman riot' is quoted by Isobel Murray on page 149. Murray quotes Kesson's,'It was only when I began to break a rule…' on page 84. The granddaughter's description 'dancing, kicking up her legs' is recorded on page 325.

Page 42 'High up in the shadow of the Red Rock, she…' and later 'scushing through the soft, white…' come from semi-autobiographical fiction in *I to the Hills* published in the Scots Magazine, September 1946, and quoted by Isobel Murray in *Jessie Kesson – Writing her Life* (page 137-8).

Page 43 'Keeping Away from the Water', was published in my first short story collection *Life Drawing*, (Neil Wilson Publishing, 2000).

Page 43 Eona Macnicol's 'The Small Herdsman' was anthologised in *The Devil and the Giro - The Scottish Short Story*, Ed Carl MacDougall, (Canongate, 1989).

Page 44 Jessie Kesson's 'Until Such Times' was also anthologised in *The Devil and the Giro* (above).

Page 45 *The Childhood*, Jessie Kesson's radio play from which I quote, is collected in *Somewhere Beyond – A Jessie Kesson Companion*, Ed. Isobel Murray (B&W Publishing, 2000).

Page 46 'following her all the way to Corbie's wood, and echoing …' from *Where the Apple Ripens* (page 42), Jessie Kesson (B&W Publishing, 2000).

Page 46 'Rainie Rainie Rattlestanes…' is from *The Useless One* collected in *Somewhere Beyond* (as above).

Page 47 John McCarthy described the marvel of 'walking into a cathedral…' I heard him say this on the BBC Radio 4 programme, *Excess Baggage*, 13/2/10.

Page 49 'her sense of being an outsider…' from Isobel Murray's introduction to *Somewhere Beyond*, Jessie Kesson (B&W Publishing 2000).

Ways of life

Page 51 Christina Foyle, owner of Foyles bookshop, wrote 'crazy, wild and full of panache' in a letter written in March 1978 to Ledig-Rowohlt which is on display in the Château.

Page 52 Ahdaf Soueif's keynote speech at Edinburgh can be found here: www.edinburghworldwritersconference.org/should-literature-be-political/ahdaf-soueif/

Stairway to Heaven?

Page 59 Hamish Fulton, walking artist: www.hamish-fulton.com

Page 62 *The Ornament of the World – How Muslims, Jews and Christians Created a Culture of Tolerance in Medieval Spain* by Maria Rosa Menocal (Back Bay Books, 2002) was a fascinating read in relation to the history of Al-Andalus. I have quoted from pages 34, 'these libraries were the monuments of a culture that treasured…';18, 'loving cultivation – some would say adoration…'; 274 , 'the hope that stories can bring…'

Page 62 The information about paper making in Játiva can be found here: www.thespanishdream.com/pages/EN/articles.php

Page 63 'A Common Word between Us and You' is an ongoing initiative reported on here www.acommonword.com/ where the original letter can also be read.

Page 63 *Ghosts of Spain – Travels Through a Country's Hidden Past* by Giles Tremlett (Faber & Faber, 2006).

Page 63 The situation of expatriate occupation referred to has obviously altered considerably since the economic crash. Spain's coasts are now dubbed the 'Costa Catastrophe' as hundreds of thousands of new homes remain unsold.

Page 64 Prize-winning British poet Christopher North and his wife Marisa Lillo-Verdú, an *Alicantina* by birth, opened the Almassera Vella (or Old Olive Press) in 2002 as a centre for retreats and residential courses. The annual programme of writing, walking, art and occasional cookery can be found here: www.oldolivepress.com

Page 66 *The Road to Oxiana* by Robert Byron (Penguin Classics, 2007). I have quoted from pages: 7, '…over the whole scene hangs…'; 200, 'one third of the adult male population…';

318, 'The getting up at four, …'; 170, 'Seen from behind, the castle…'. The photograph on the book's cover described on page [66] is by A T Wilson, 1911.

Page74 The miniature fern palm referred to is Chamaerops humilis - the only indigenous palm tree in Europe.

Page 75 'Yet the UN estimates that the entire number…' I took this information from an article by Maya Jaggi published in November 2007: www.theguardian.com/books/2007/nov/17/featuresreviews.guardianreview3 and further detailed background can be found in a Literature Across Frontiers report from December 2011, *Literary Translation From Arabic Into English In The United Kingdom And Ireland, 1990-2010* by Alexandra Büchler and Alice Guthrie, available online here: www.lafpublications.files.wordpress.com/2011/04/literary-translation-from-arabic-into-english-in-the-united-kingdom-and-ireland-1990-2010-final3.pdf The interest in translation from Arabic works into English has grown considerably since the start of the Arab Spring.

Islamic Science and Engineering by Donald R Hill (Edinburgh University Press, 1994) was useful background reading.

Baring our Soles

Page 91 *Daughters of the Glen* by Alexandra Stewart, (Leura Press, Aberfeldy, 1987)

Page 94 *The First Light – The Story of Innerpeffray Library* by George Chamier (The Library of Innerpeffray, 2009). www.innerpeffraylibrary.co.uk

Philo Ikonya, writer and activist, left Kenya in late 2009 to be hosted in Oslo, Norway, which is part of the International Cities of Refuge

Network. See more here: www.icorn.org and www.philoikonya.com

Pappa's Shoes

Page 103 '...People should be encouraged to walk in the hills. It will increase their attachment to their country.' From *Palestinian Walks*, by Raja Shehadeh, (Profile Books, 2007). This book won the Orwell Prize in 2008 and shows how Raja's life as a writer, human rights lawyer and peace activist, and the fate of the landscape are intertwined. It is an intensely personal account of life in one of the world's most troubled regions, and a poignant exploration of what so many of us take for granted – the freedom to roam the countryside.

Page 104 Extracts from Sven Sømme's own writing in this chapter come from his original book 'Biologist on the Run' republished as *Another Man's Shoes*, Sven Sømme (Polperro Heritage Press, 2005). It includes a fascinating account of Norway under occupation as well as the story of his arrest and escape. His daughter Ellie Sømme provides in it an account of the commemorative journey across Norway in 2004.

Page 118 'Naismith's Rule' was devised in 1892 by William W. Naismith, a Scot, and allows a rough calculation to be made of the time a walk will take, allowing one hour for every five kilometres (3.1 miles) forward, plus 1 hour for every 600 metres (2,000 ft) of ascent.

Outlasting our Tracks

Page 129 The epigram 'the wonderful and terrible …', and quotes 'The arête… rises from the glacier…', and 'It's not nice to carry…', come from *Letters of Gertrude Bell Vol I,* (Ernest Benn Ltd, 1927).

Page 134 'the footmark, so to speak, of a glacier is…' *Modern painters, Part V Mountain Beauty,* John Ruskin 1856.

Page 140 'Climb if you will…' from *Scrambles Amongst the Alps 1860-1869,* Edward Whymer (National Geographic Adventure Classics, 2002).

Whilst in Switzerland on this adventure I was reading *The Tenderness of Wolves* by Stef Penney (Quercus, 2006). The huge snowscapes it evoked extended the environment I was in. I was very taken by an observation near the end of the novel about the epic trails characters made though the snow: 'Every so often I see a print that I know is mine… This country is scored with such marks; slender traces of human desire. But these trails, like this bitter path, are fragile, winterworn and when the snow falls again or when it thaws in spring, all trace of our passing will vanish. Even so, three of these tracks have outlasted the men who made them'.

Robert Macfarlane's *Mountains of the Mind* (Granta, 2003) was a great companion read for the experiences of this chapter, and for its writing.

The heaven above and the road below

The title is taken from Robert Louis Stevenson's *The Vagabond.* This is an extract:

> 'Let the blow fall soon or late,
> Let what will be o'er me;
> Give the face of earth around,
> And the road before me.

Wealth I ask not, hope nor love,
Nor a friend to know me;
All I ask, the heaven above
And the road below me.'

Page 158 '...the great affair is to move; to...' from *Travels with a Donkey in the Cévennes,* Robert Louis Stevenson, 1879.

The Return of Hoof Beats

Page 165 *The Herding Rune from South Uist* as quoted to the Napier Commission by Alexander Carmichael, is referred to by Rob Gibson in *Plaids and Bandanas* (Luath Press, 2003).

Page 167 Out of the joint experience of canoeing the river Spey in 2000, a dynamic network known as SpeyGrian (Gaelic for 'sun on the Spey') arose, based in Scotland but drawing in members from other continents. Since then SpeyGrian has thrived and transformed with a focus on learning through outdoor journeys and a programme including professional development for Scottish teachers. www.speygrian.org.uk

Page 167 Whilst on her incredible journey from Dunvegan to Smithfield Market, Vyv Wood-Gee somehow managed to keep a blog: www.droversfootsteps.blogspot.co.uk

Page 168 *The Drove Roads of Scotland,* A.R.B. Haldane, (Birlinn, 1997) was an important source for this and the following chapter. I've quoted here from page 24, 'the highways which distress...'

Page 169 Alexandra Stewart's account of her father's walk appears in her memoir, *Daughters of the Glen,* (Leura Press, Aberfeldy, 1986).

Page 175 *Highland Highways – Old Roads in Atholl* by John Kerr, (John Donald Publishers Ltd,1991) is an invaluable guide to the lore and history of the old ways in this area and was where I read about the drovers' gathering place on Choire Bhran.

Joyce Gilbert, Education Officer for the Royal Scottish Geographical Society who organised this journey has now developed a major educational project on the topic of droving called 'Stories in the Land.' www.storiesintheland.blogspot.co.uk/

The Dogs' Route

Page 183 Prose poem *In Praise of Walking*, by Thomas A Clark (Moschatel Press, 2004).

Page 184 The information about dogs returning alone appears in *The Drove Roads of Scotland*, A.R.B. Haldane, (Birlinn, 1997) page 26. I have quoted from pages: 77, 'To one watching from the hill overlooking…'; and 24, special qualities of 'head, heart and body'.

Page 188 'Another long-distance solo walker I've come…' This was Daryl May. I also love the way he invented characters who he 'met' in various pubs, resuming conversations along the way. This is his blog: www.mylongwalk.com

Page 190 *Recollections of a Tour Made in Scotland 1803*, by Dorothy Wordsworth (publ.1874). Available as an e-book from www.undiscoveredscotland.com

Page 191 My story referred to here is 'The Weight of the Earth and the Lightness of the Human Heart', in *The Searching Glance*, (Salt, 2008), also broadcast as a reading for BBC Radio 4.

Page 199 Uamh An Ard Achadh (Cave of the High Field or High Pasture Cave) is an ongoing archaeological project of great significance. See more here: www.high-pasture-cave.org/

Page 209 *Loch Coruisk, Skye*, JMW Turner (1831) is in the National Galleries of Scotland collection and can be viewed online: www.nationalgalleries.org

Page 211 Ben Okri's image of the writer dropping a fishing line into the unconscious was referred to in a column by Roselle Angwin in Mslexia magazine edition 35. His essays in *A Way of Being Free* (Phoenix, 1998) also explore the topic of creativity.

To be a Pilgrim

Page 221 The book I referred to on the Eildon Hills was *St Cuthbert's Way – A Pilgrims' Companion,* by Mary Low (Wild Goose Publications, 1999), which has historical and folkloric background for the pilgrim.

Page 227 Another book I enjoyed as background to this walk was *Fire of The North – The Life of St Cuthbert,* by David Adam (SPCK, 1993).

Page 228 My exploration of shells was enhanced by reading *The Poetics of Space,* Gaston Bachelard (Beacon Press, 1994). He speaks of shells as 'a refuge in which life is concentrated, prepared and transformed'.

Friendly Paths

Page 239 Ideas about ritualistic processions and a sense of belonging are explored by Katrin Lund in 'Listen to the Sound of Time: Walking with Saints in an Andalusian Village' in *Ways of Walking – Ethnography and Practice on Foot* edited by Tim Ingold and Lee Vergunst (Ashgate, 2008). Anyone interested in walking practice will also enjoy the other contributions to this book.

Page 243 'or perhaps, as some would say,...' It seems that 'The Birks o' Aberfeldy' may have been adapted by Burns from a traditional song from Aberdeenshire, 'The Birks of Abergeldie'.

Page 243 Dorothy Wordsworth's time in Aberfeldy is recorded in *Recollections of a Tour Made in Scotland 1803* (see above).

Page 246 'Revisiting our own memories is like this too...' Such ideas about the construction of memory are explored by writer and psychologist Charles Fernyhough in his book, *Pieces of Light - The new science of memory* (Profile Books, 2012).

Page 246 Christian McEwen refers to Grace Paley's statement in her book, *World Enough and Time – On Creativity and Slowing Down* (Bauhan Publishing, 2011). I was reading this book whilst on retreat at Lavigny and although I was working hard it was a great invitation (and practical guide) to dwelling, noticing and appreciating where I was.

I was undertaking this walking and writing project most fully from 2007 to 2009 due to a Creative Scotland Award, and during that time I kept a blog. Although largely an archive now it can still be viewed at: www.walkingandwriting.blogspot.co.uk

The single most significant and comprehensive book I read about walking was *Wanderlust* by Rebecca Solnit (Verso, 2001).

Acknowledgements

In 2007 I received a Creative Scotland Award from the Scottish Arts Council to explore a number of paths with my feet and in words. This book is one of the outcomes of that project and parts of it have already appeared elsewhere. An extract from *The Dogs' Route* with the title *Cailliche* was anthologised in 'Cleave - New writing by women in Scotland', Two Ravens Press, 2008. A slightly different version of *Baring Our Soles* appeared in the Tramway's online magazine Algebra in May 2011 with the title *The Heart in Our Soles.* I published the two essays in the section *Following Our Fathers* in a small book of that name in 2012. (Under the same 'best foot books' imprint two further walking stories not included in this book are: *Whiter than White* and *The Beat of Heart Stones*). *The Return of Hoof Beats* was published in Earthlines magazine in March 2014.

I'm indebted to many people who have been involved in this project in different ways over its long course. I had some wonderful walking companions many of whom are mentioned in the text. Others who walked with me or helped with logistics included: Renée Mboya, Monica Ikonya, Phil Horey, the Sømme family in Britain and Norway (as well as a wonderful chain of Norwegian hosts), Rick Worrell, Colin Hughes, Gill Russell, Charlotte Flower, Sue Atkinson and Iain MacGowan.

Others who assisted my research, discussed ideas and/or encouraged me included Dee Heddon, Tom Pow, Robert Macfarlane, Andrew Ross ex-president of the Oxford University Mountaineering Club, Marian Dawson, Anne Colman, my uncle Martin Cracknell and mother Jenny Scanlan.

I had some superb readers of drafts of these essays in Jamie Grant, Polly Pullar, Ruary Mackenzie Dodds and Ruth Atkinson. Travel writer John Harrison also provided a very useful commentary on an earlier draft of the book via The Literary Consultancy.

The month I spent at an international writers retreat at Lavigny in 2012 was an invaluable asset to finishing the book and I'd like to thank my hosts and fellow writers for their support and for tolerating my daily wanderings.

And finally for making this book happen I'd like to thank my agent Jenny Brown and the great team at Freight Books.

For permission to quote extracts from these works, thanks to :
Claire Tomalin and David Godwin Associates for *Thomas Hardy, The Time-Torn Man* by Claire Tomalin (Penguin, 2007).

Isobel Murray for: *Jessie Kesson – Writing her Life* (Canongate 2000); and her introduction to *Somewhere Beyond*, by Jessie Kesson, (B+W Publishing 2000).

Johnson & Alcock Ltd for the following works by Jessie Kesson: *A Country Dweller's Years – Nature writings by Jessie Kesson*, Ed. Isobel Murray (Kennedy and Boyd, 2009); *I to the Hills* published in the Scots Magazine, September 1946; *Where the Apple Ripens*, Jessie Kesson (B&W Publishing, 2000); 'The Useless One' and 'The Childhood' collected in *Somewhere Beyond – A Jessie Kesson Companion,* Ed. Isobel Murray (B&W Publishing, 2000).

Thomas A Clark for his prose poem, *In Praise of Walking.*

Keith Macbeath for *Daughters of the Glen* by Alexandra Stewart. The book remains available for sale from Leura Press, 1 Alma Avenue, Aberfeldy, Perthshire PH15 2BW - £10 (plus postage and packing £2.50 UK, £5 overseas).

Ellie Sømme for *Another Man's Shoes*, Sven Sømme (Polperro Heritage Press, 2005).

Birlinn Ltd for *The Drove Roads of Scotland*, A.R.B. Haldane, (Birlinn, 1997).

Raja Shehadeh for his *Palestinian Walks* (Profile Books, 2007).

All efforts have been made to seek permission from relevant parties to reproduce quoted work contained in this book. No work has been reproduced without seeking appropriate permissions.

Photograph of Jessie Kesson reproduced with kind permission of the Herald newspaper.